IPHONE 11 PRO MAX
USERS GUIDE
AND PHOTOGRAPHY

An Easy to Follow Guide to Master the Camera App on
Your iPhone 11 & iPhone 11 Pro Max and Shoot Cinematic
Videos

GW00480766

PABLO
MENDOZA

Disclaimer

The information in this book is based on personal experience and anecdotal evidence. Although the author has made every attempt to achieve an accuracy of the information gathered in this book, they make no representation or warranties concerning the accuracy or completeness of the contents of this book. Your circumstances may not be suited to some illustrations in this book.

The author disclaims any liability arising directly or indirectly from the use of this book. Readers are encouraged to seek accounting, legal, or professional help when required.

This guide is for informational purposes only, and the author does not accept any responsibilities for any liabilities resulting from the use of this information. While every attempt has been made to verify the information provided here, the author cannot assume any responsibility for errors, inaccuracies, or omission.

TABLE OFCONTENTS

INTRODUCTION

The iPhone 11 Pro-Max became available for preorder on September 13, 2019; the new device prices range depending on the storage capacity. The phone models three different storage capacity and different prices; the 64GB model is available at $1099, while the 256GB model is available at $1249, and finally, the 512GB model is currently staked at $1449.

Though the latest iPhone 11 Pro-Max does not look much different from its others accomplice, according to apple, it is made from the most hardened glass ever in a smartphone and offer improved water resistance(IP68) which boost overall durability, the spatial audio support provides a more immersive sound experience, and Dolby Atmos is supported.

The top performance of a phone has always been a perfect shot for a great smartphone, and the best leading divisions of Smartphones are flaunting their super high tech display, Apple is not lagging in keeping up with trends and also in exceeding tech performance.

This book is designed to promote iPhone 11 Pro Max user guide and photography so that consumers, reviewers, and journalists would all recognize, appreciate and get in the know of all

The benefits they stand to get in purchasing this advanced smartphone.

CHAPTER ONE

What's New in IOS 13?

The iPhone 11 Pro-Max operates the latest iOS interface, which is the iOS 13.

The new iOS 13 as upgraded some new features in its interface and other services, these are few new things found in the new iOS 13:

Camera

The portrait lighting now allows you to virtually adjust the intensity of each studio lighting effect, although a unique lighting effect with high key light mono, creates a beautiful look with a gray-scale subject on a white background.

You can also apply a depth field effect that keeps subjects (humans) and object (things) sharp while creating a beautifully blurred background.

Apply and adjust different effects to your portrait mode photos, and with a True-Depth camera, taking a Selfie in portrait mode is obtainable.

Dark-Mode

There's now a new DARK-MODE feature that gives the entire iOS experience a fantastic dark color scheme, which is perfect for lowlights environment.

You can turn on the DARK-MODE feature from around the control center or decide to set it, to turn on at night automatically.

The incredible usefulness of this feature is that the light emanating from your device won't worry people close to you.

How to use and adjust the DARK-MODE feature will be discussed later in this guide.

Maps

This Application has been upgraded with more realistic details for roads, beaches, parks, and buildings. You can now explore where you're going even before you get there

Siri

The new Siri voice sound is an incredible feature, which now speaks longer phrases than before, the Siri feature also offers personalized suggestions when you search in podcast, safari, and maps.

The feature can detect reminders in messages; more about Siri will be discussed later in this guide.

There are plenty of updated features found in iOS 13; all features will be discussed thoroughly in this guide with photos for in-depth understanding.

Get Started

You need to set up your new iPhone 11 Pro-Max using the internet, or you set it up by connecting to your personal computer.

To make your setup process very easy, you'll need to have the following items listed below;

1. A working Internet connection, a Wi-Fi network is advisable; however, you'll need the username as well as the password of that particular Network.

2. An Apple ID as well as password, if you lack one, you'll need to create one; this can be done during the setup.

3. Your credit or debit card should be available if only you like to add a card to apple pay during set up. NB: This is optional

4. You may also need your previous iPhone if you have one of your devices only if you're transferring old data to your new device.

5. If you were using Android previously, you might need the device to be able to transfer your android contents to iPhone

Now that you've all the listed above based on how you want to set up, you can now follow the procedures below;

A. Tap and press the side button until the Apple icon/logo appears on the screen. NB: If your iPhone doesn't come up, you may need to plug in the charger to boost battery.

B. After that, perform one of the following;

1. Once the iPhone comes up, Tap SETUP MANUALLY, then use on-screen instructions.

Do you have an old iPhone or iPod touch with iOS 11, iPad os13, or later, if so, you have the option of QUICK START to automatically setup your device?

For Manual setup without transferring of old data follow this procedure listed below;

1. Tap SETUP AS NEW IPHONE

2. Provide Apple ID with Password. If you lack one, quickly create a new one by tapping the "DON'T, HAVE AN APPLE ID" option and use the instructions that follow.

3. Read and understand before agreeing to Apple's terms and conditions

4. Tap agree to confirm

5. Setup APPLE PAY by following the instructions (NB: This will be discussed in details later in this chapter)

Now, if you have a previous iPhone or Android and would like to transfer old files to your newly bought iPhone 11 pro-max, you'll need to use the QUICK START setup process.

If either devices have iOS 12.4, ipados13, or subsequent, you can transfer your data wirelessly from your other device to the recent one.

QUICKSTART offers the option of using iPhone migration; this allows you to send all your data wirelessly from your former iPhone to your new one.

How to make use of quickstart

1. Switch on your latest device and place it close to your old one, which is using iOS 11 or later; the quick start screen will pop up on the previous iPhone, and it will bring up an option of using Apple ID to set up your new device. Make sure the ID you are using is the correct one, TAP CONTINUE. If somehow you don't see the option to continue on your old device, make sure the Bluetooth is turned on.

2. Hold on till something like an animation pops up on the screen of your new device, place your previous device on top of the latest one, let the animation be in the center of the viewfinder, Hold on till you see a pop up that says "Finish on New Device." If eventually, your old device camera doesn't work, TAP AUTHENTICATE MANUALLY, adhere to the on-screen instructions that come up.

3. Enter your old device passcode when the option pops up.

4. Face ID can be set up with the instructions provided on your latest device.

5. When the option comes on, you can type your Apple ID.

6. Now your new device will ask you whether to restore your data from your current iCloud backup or update your old device's backup before restoring. After you have selected a backup, you can choose to

transfer some settings that are related to location, apple pay, and Siri. However, if you decide to update your device, make sure WIFI is enabled on your device.

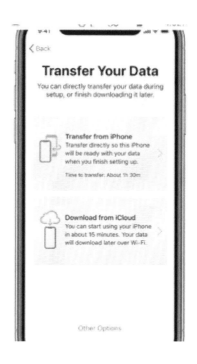

Haptic Touch Feature

This is a unique feature that was used in replacing the 3D touch; the haptic feature can be expressed when you make a touch and hold gesture on your device screen to access additional options within apps and iOS.

The feature first appeared in the iPhone XR. However, it offered limited use in iOS 12. When the iOS 13, as well as the iPhone 11 series, were launched, apple expanded the haptic touch options and replaced it with the 3D touch in iPhone 11 pro-max.

Although there were rumors that users weren't happy when the 3D touch that was changed to Haptic touch in the iPhone 11 series, however, apple believes haptic touch offers the same experience with the 3D touch without needing the additional pressure sensitivity and hardware the 3D touch required.

Haptic touch feature allows you to use long presses to access popup menus that offer quick actions. Using some apps, you can even peek into the app's content. However, Apple may update haptic touch features in years to come.

It's easy to manipulate the time needed to activate haptic touch whenever you use a touch and hold gesture.

To adjust haptic touch settings, follow the steps below;

- Tap SETTINGS, scroll down to ACCESSIBILITY, tap TOUCH, then select HAPTIC TOUCH
- Select whether you want fast or slow
- If you're going to make a rapid test, Tap the flower or flashlight icon under the touch duration test.

Dust and Water Resist

The latest iPhone 11 Pro-Max has an IP68 water resistance rating, but it is more water-resistant, it has been experimented to survive a depth of four meters(13 feet) for about half an hour, which is a massive improvement since the introduction of the iPhone x and 11 which allows only 2 meters depth range respectively.

According to the IP68 number, the six refers to dust resistance, which means the iPhone 11 Pro-Max can hold up to dust, dirt, and other particulates.

The IP68 water resistance can stand splashes, rainfall, and little mistaken water exposure, however intentional water exposure should be avoided if possible.

Apple had warned that dust and water-resistant are temporary conditions and will deteriorate as a result of normal wear.

The Neural Engine

A13 new chip contains an 8-core motor neuron next generation; Apple says it's speedy to analyze photos and videos in real-time.

The CPU is now six times faster because of the pair of machine learning accelerators, delivering more than one trillion operations every second.

The neural engine is 20% quicker and will only consume 15% power than the former generation neural engine.

According to apple, the neural engine powers the camera system face ID, AR apps, and more.

CHAPTER TWO

Ram and Storage

The iPhone 11 Pro-Max has a 4GB Random access memory (RAM), which is available to apps and iOS systems; this makes the device very fast and swift in performing tasks, with the amount of RAM available the devices we rarely hang, although when the pressure of background apps is too much, freezing may occur.

The storage of the iPhone 11 Pro-Max varies just as the price changes; the iPhone 11 pro max has three different types of storage capacity models; it has the 64GB model, 256GB model, and the 512GB model, each model varies in price.

How to Use Virtual Trackpad

The virtual trackpad was a feature that was related to the 3D touch; the feature allows you to move the cursor on the screen through a particular text you have written down. The gesture is popular because it will enable you to make quick edits without having to scroll up and tap the display.

However, Apple has replaced the 3D touch feature with the new haptic touch feature changing the way the virtual trackpad functions slightly.

Using the virtual trackpad in the iPhone 11 pro-max, you have to tap and hold the spacebar to bring up the trackpad; you should note that tapping and holding anywhere on the keyboard no longer works.

If you tried activating the virtual trackpad the old way, it wouldn't work, how to enable it has been explained above.

How to Insert SIM Card

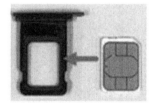

Before you insert your SIM card, please read and understand the following precautions carefully;

❖ Never attempt to add or remove the SIM card while the device is on, if care is not taking, the act may harm the SIM card or the device.

❖ Never modify or alter your SIM card.

Now that you've seen the precautions, you can now follow the steps below to insert your SIM card;

1. Make sure the device is powered off.

2. Remove the tray for the SIM-card, which is on the edge of the SIM-card tray, using the tool to release the SIM-card or a clamp, insert it into the slot.

3. The SIM card on the SIM card tray should be in place (**NB:** Nano-SIM and the gold chip should be facing up)

4. Push the SIM card tray back inside, press it hard to lock into place.

NB: When replacing SIM cards, make sure you remove the existing SIM first before inserting the new one. However, the iPhone 11 Pro-Max features dual SIM support.

How to Adjust Brightness and Color

On your iPhone 11 pro-max, you can save battery life, when you dim the screen use night mode, by setting dark mode and automatically adjust the screen for your lighting conditions and preferences.

The feature 'Dark Mode' gives the entire iPhone a dark color scheme, which is perfect in environments with low light. Dark mode can be controlled in the center, or you can make it come up at night, with Dark-mode automatically turned on; you can read in bed without disturbing anybody next to you.

To turn on Dark-mode, do any of the following steps below;

❖ Launch the control center, touch and hold the sun like an icon, then tap the half colored circle to turn on Dark-mode.

❖ Open settings App, locate DISPLAY AND BRIGHTNESS tap on it, and now select dark to turn on Dark-mode or select light to turn it off, if it was previously activated.

You can easily schedule Dark-mode to turn off and on automatically. To achieve this, follow these simple steps below;

1. Launch the Settings app, scroll to DISPLAY AND BRIGHTNESS, then tap on it.
2. Activate automatic, then tap options
3. Choose from either sunset to sunrise or custom schedule

If you selected a custom schedule, tap the options to schedule the times you want the dark mode to turn on and turn off; however, if you selected sunset to sunrise, iPhone will use the data from your clock and geolocation to determine when it's the night for you.

You can save the battery life of your device by making the screen dimmer; you can do these by performing one of the following steps below;

❖ Open control center, then drag the sun-like icon

❖ Launch Settings app, scroll to DISPLAY AND BRIGHTNESS, and drag the slider.

The iPhone adjusts the brightness of the screen automatically for the light condition; it uses the built-in ambient light sensor.

To activate the automatic screen adjust, follow these two steps below;

1. Launch Settings app and tap on ACCESSIBILITY
2. Select DISPLAY AND TEXT SIZE, and then choose AUTO BRIGHTNESS.

The True Tone is a light feature that adapts the color and intensity of the display to match the light in your environment.

To activate True Tone, do any of the following listed below;

❖ Open control center, press and hold the sun-like icon, then tap the ash-colored sun-like icon to turn on True Tone or off.

❖ Launch the Settings app, tap on DISPLAY AND BRIGHTNESS, select True Tone to either turn on or off.

Nightshift is a light feature that helps you when you're in a dark room in the day time, to activate the nightshift feature, use the procedure below;

❖ Open control center, touch and hold the sun-like icon, then tap the sun like icon painted half

How to View Photos, Videos and As Well Edit Them

To view photos, you are to use the photos app, and you can see the video there as well, browse your photos, albums memories, and more using **the photo, albums, search tabs, and for your options.**

❖ *Photos:* You can browse your photos and videos, well organized by days, months, and years.

❖ *For you:* This personalized feed shows your memories, featured photos, shared albums, and more.

❖ *Albums:* You can view the albums you created or shared, your photos are organized by album

Categories- e.g., people and places, and media types.

❖ **Search:** Type in the search filed to either search for photos by date, place, location, or whatever that's in them.

The photos and videos on your iPhone 11 Pro-Max are well organized by years, months, days, and all images in the photo tab. You can find your best shot in previous years, posts throwbacks in months go through the photographs, to browse your photos, tap the photos' tab, then select any of the following listed below:

❖ **Years:** locate a specific year in your photo library and see significant moments highlighted in a slideshow.

❖ **Months:** You can view collections of some photos that you took months ago, organized by significant events, like social occasions and family outing.

❖ **Days:** You can view your photos in chronological order, arranged by the time or place the photo was taken.

❖ **All photos:** Here, you can view all of your photos and videos; you can pinch to zoom in and out to see your pictures and library in the detail you want.

categories to help you find the
photo you're looking for.

In checking out a photo in full screen, you can zoom in or out; to get this, you need to double-tap or pinch out to zoom in after you have zoomed, drag to see other parts of the photo. Double-tap again or pinch close to zoom out.

To share the photo while viewing it on the full screen, tap the arrow icon; you can also add to favorites by tapping the love icon.

To delete a photo, tap the photo or video to display in full screen, then tap the waste bin icon, (**NB:** deleted pictures and videos will be stored in the recently deleted album for 30 days, where you can either recover them or permanently delete them from your device.

To hide photos, tap the arrow key while viewing pictures in full screen, then tap HIDE in the list of options. (**NB:** hidden photos are all moved to a hidden album, there's nowhere you can view them again in the device)

You can also recover deleted photos, or you can permanently delete them, to perform any of the stated functions, do the below:

1. Open the Albums tab, then select Recent Delete under OTHER ALBUMS
2. Tap SELECT, then choose the videos or photo you want to delete or recover
3. Select RECOVER or DELETE below the iPhone screen.

When browsing through the photo library in the photos lab, regular videos will auto-play when you come across them; you can tap a video to begin playing it in full screen without sound. To perform the function, do any of the following;

❖ Open the player controls below the video to pause, play, un-mute, and mute; touch the screen to hide the player controls.

❖ You can double-tap the screen to toggle between full screen and fit to screen.

A slideshow can be created; a slideshow is a collection of your photos, which is formatted and set with music. To create a slideshow, do follow these simple steps below;

1. Open the photos tab
2. View your photos using the ALL PHOTOS option or DAYS, then tap select;
3. Select each photo you want to use in the slideshow, when done, tap the arrow-like icon.
4. A list of options will appear, tap slideshow.
5. Touch the screen, and then tap options in the bottom right to alter the slideshow theme, music, and more.

Now let's move to the editing of photos and videos, you can edit your pictures in the Photos app using the tools installed in it. Using iCloud photos saves any edit you make across all your devices if you have more than one.

Adjusting the color and light in a photo is simple, to do so follow these steps listed below;

1. Open the photos app and tap a picture or video thumbnail to view it in full screen.

2. Select edit, then swipe to the left under the photo to reveal the editing buttons for each effect, such as brilliance, highlight, and exposure.

3. Tap on a button, then drag the slider to adjust the effect to your taste (**NB:** The adjustment level you make for each effect will be displayed by the outline around the button, now you can see from a glance which effects have been increased or decreased.)

4. To compare the effected photo from the un-affected one, tap the chosen button, and visualize the shot before and after the effect is applied, tap the photo to toggle between the edited version and the original.

(NB: you can tap the magic wand icon to edit your photos or videos with effects automatically)

To CROP, ROTATE OR FLIP A PHOTO, you'll have to follow these simple steps listed below;

1. Open the photos app then tap on a photo or video thumbnail to view it in full screen.
2. Select Edit then tap the crop icon, after that, do any of the following;

❖ ***Crop Manually:*** Drag the four rectangle corners to crop the area you want to keep in the photo, or you pinch the picture open or closed.

❖ ***Crop to a standard preset Ratio:*** Tap the rectangle-like icon, then you can insert the preferred number ratio you wish to crop your photo to, e.g., 2:3, 8:10, and more.

❖ Tap the rectangle icon with an arrow key at the top to rotate your photo in degrees.

❖ Tap the right-angled triangle backing each other with an arrow on top to flip the image horizontally.

3. When you are done, tap Done to save your edits, or if you don't like your changes, tap CANCEL, then tap DISCARD CHANGES.

To apply specific filter effects, you'll need to follow these steps below;

1. Open the photos app then tap a photo or video thumbnail to view it in full screen
2. Select edit, then tap the three closed circle to apply various filter effects, e.g., Vivid, Silver-tone, and Dramatic.
3. For the adjustment of the effect, select a filter and drag slider.

4. If you wish to compare the original photo with the edited photo, tap the photo.

5. Tap DONE, save your edits, or if not satisfied with the changes, tap CANCEL, then Tap DISCARD CHANGES

The last thing we would be looking at in this topic would be VIDEO TRIMMING; to trim videos, please follow these simple steps listed below;

1. Open the photos app, select a video, tap to edit.
2. Drag the frame viewer's end, tap 'Done.'
3. Touch 'save video' to save trimmed video, To save both versions of the video, tap 'save video as a new clip.'

The trim can be undone after saving; to do this, open the video, then Tap EDIT, then select REVERT.

CHAPTER THREE

iPhone 11 Pro For Photography

The new iPhone 11 Pro Max is a powerful camera that also has the functions of a smartphone. With its three lenses camera, fast A13 Bionic processor with artificial intelligence, and remarkable battery life - the new iPhone is packed with the latest technology, which should be particularly interesting for photographers. While earlier smartphone photos on vacation were nothing more than pixelated snapshots for the private collection, the iPhone X and comparable models from other manufacturers at the latest, high-quality images can be taken while traveling and, of course, in everyday life. The advantages of smartphone photography are apparent: the gadgets are always there. With the new smartphone from Apple and the 12-megapixel triple camera with ultra-wide-angle, wide-angle, and telephoto lens, a new era of photography is being heralded. What does the new smartphone do? And in the future, will only smartphone photography be enough on vacation and travel? In the book, we checked the iPhone 11 Pro Max photography intensively and introduced you to all the strengths and weaknesses of the device camera in everyday life, during sports and especially when traveling and on vacation. Because where better to use the triple camera than in the most beautiful travel destinations in the world?

iPhone 11 Pro Max is excellently manufactured (compared to some predecessors) and immediately catches the eye with its matte back, which according to the manufacturer, is particularly hard and robust - ideal conditions for everyone who wants to use the smartphone properly while traveling and on vacation. The size and weight of the Max version with a 6.5-inch display are, of course, immediately noticeable. For its size, the new device is surprisingly comfortable to hold. After all, with all outdoor tours, adventures, and active holidays, the smartphone you take with you must be handy and compact.

Camera Review

iPhone 11 Pro Max camera has been described as the best cameras currently installed in a smartphone after some extensive test we can only agree that the image quality is simply brilliant.

With its super Retina display, Apple's latest A13 Bionic chipset, and up to 512 GB of internal storage, is also the first iPhone with a triple camera configuration. In addition to the primary wide-angle camera and the telephoto camera (both of which have the same focal length as the previous XS Max), the phone is now equipped with an ultra-wide-angle camera with an equivalent 13mm field of view.

In terms of image processing, the new Deep Fusion technology uses the chipset's neural engine and advanced machine learning technology to perform pixel-by-pixel optimization to obtain better textures, less noise, and a more excellent dynamic range. Read our full review to learn how the new components of this phone work together.

The triple camera makes a promising impression at first glance and conveys the feeling of having a professional camera in your hand for taking high-quality photos. The early recordings with the new high-end smartphone are brilliant. The smartphone takes razor-sharp pictures in daylight; this is mainly due to the new Deep Fusion technology, which calculates the result from several individual images. In the dark, the new night mode switches on, with which high-quality and professional night pictures can be taken even in complete darkness; this happens, by exposing the images for up to ten seconds. All in all, the first impression of the photography options is clear: Especially when it comes to the performance of the three cameras, the iPhone 11 Pro Max deserves the name Pro.

Main camera Specifications

Main camera: 12-megapixel 1 / 2.55-inch sensor, f /1.8 lens, 26 mm equivalent focal length, optical image stabilization (OIS), phase detection autofocus (PDAF)

Ultra-wide-angle lens: 12-megapixel sensor, f/2.4 lens, 13 mm equivalent focal length

Telephoto lens: 12MP 1/ 3.4-inch sensor, f/2.0 lens, 52mm equivalent focal length, optical image stabilization (OIS), phase detection autofocus (PDAF)

4-LED dual color flash

4K video, 2160p / 60fps (default 1080p / 30fps)

Camera Highlight

Let's not spend much time talking about cameras iPhone 11 Pro Max. Each phone has four cameras - three at the back and one at the front.

The rear camera consists of three cameras:

• 12-megapixel "wide" camera with aperture f /1.8 optical aperture (OIS) aperture

• 12-megapixel "2x zoom [telephoto]" camera f / 2.0 aperture with OIS

• 12-megapixel "ultra-wide" camera with f / 2.4 aperture and 120-degree field of view

Inside the box, the "TrueDepth" camera has been updated from the iPhone XS 7 megapixel shooter to a 12-megapixel camera with an aperture of f / 2.2.

If you have an iPhone with a single camera on the back, you might think that the iPhone 11 Pro three-camera system is a little too much. But I think when you use it and see how the three cameras work like one, giving you zoom ranges from 13mm (very wide) to 26mm (wide) to 52mm (2x zoom), you won't be able to turn back in one lens. You'll get slightly better shots, especially in small scenes, with a 2x zoom lens because it has a faster f / 2.0 aperture to capture more light, but a super-wide camera is the star attraction.

Apple isn't the first to have included a three-camera system with an ultra-wide lens. Huawei has beaten everyone to break through the 20 pro mate, and this year almost all the phone manufacturers, including Samsung and OnePlus, have added their flagship phones to correct the Triple rear cameras.

In typical Apple style, however, the company admitted the first to focus on creating a better three-camera system. Other phones may have a similar three-camera system, but it will not work consistently.

The ultra-wide camera is so fun to shoot.

Deep Apple software related to camera hardware is the device that distinguishes the iPhone 11 Pro Max's camera and makes zooming between the three cameras so smooth; There is no stuttering that you see on an Android phone when you switch from one camera to another.

For this reason, the three cameras on the back of the iPhone 11 Pro are aligned as they are: for direct zoom from the middle. On Android phones, where the three cameras are usually aligned in sequence, you have to physically move the phone left or right to reconnect photos, making it less desirable to zoom in and out and more like switching to a separate camera. It's a small detail, but if you are serious about photography, it makes all the difference.

CHAPTER FOUR

Camera Ranking

Apple iPhone 11 Pro Max scored an overall score of 117 points on the DXOMARK Camera, ranking among the top 5 in current rankings. The phone scored 124 points in photos, ranked among the best in still images, and it topped the championship with the Xiaomi Mi CC9 Pro Exclusive Edition video.

Images and Textures

The camera performed very well in quite a few areas, but there are still some issues to overcome. Still-images usually have perfect exposure; in high light and indoor conditions, the dynamic range is vast, but in complicated scenes, you can still see some spill clipping textures. In general, the iPhone is one of the best-exposed mobile phones. Only in feeble light can it perform worse than a phone with a larger image sensor (for example, Huawei Mate 30 Pro). Like previous generations of iPhones, the 11 Pro Max also scores high in color and is one of the best-performing phones in this category under all lighting conditions. In some indoor scenes and when tested in a laboratory, the phone has a slightly greenish color cast, but the overall color is usually very pleasing, while the somewhat yellowish color cast brings some touch of warmth, and this color cast is also very suitable for skin tones in portraits. The images were taken by iPhone 11 Pro Max usually shows good exposure, wide dynamic range, and pleasing color rendering.

Because Apple's new Deep Fusion uses machine learning to improve the demosaic effect, the iPhone's image details and textures have been significantly improved. The phone outlines exceptional features such as freckles, pet hair, or leaves in the distance, making it an excellent choice for landscape and portrait photography. Only in low light conditions, the iPhone details will be significantly reduced, unable to reach the level of first-class mobile phones. The phone's noise is also improved than the XS Max, but it is still noticeable in almost all light conditions. However, the image artifacts are very well controlled, with only occasional flare.

Using Camera Filters On iPhone 11 Pro Max

Camera filters offer fun ways to add a camera screen quickly, and Apple's latest iPhone 11 Pro Max is arguably the best camera package on any smartphone. With robust video recording capabilities and advanced features such as Deep Fusion photography, it is hard to beat what this Cupertino is based on technology giants. Therefore, whatever pictures we take, sometimes you want to use additional filtering features from the camera application to enhance your photography work further.

If you just upgraded to a new iPhone 11 Pro max, you might notice that filter options don't seem to be available from the Camera app. Previously, it was located in the upper-right corner of the camera application; Apple redesigned the UI to allow more features like night mode, QuickTake video, etc. Don't worry; Apple doesn't give up on filtering the way they do with 3D Touch. Instead, they move it to another location in the Camera app.

Each iPhone 11 Pro series has the same redesigned Camera app, so regardless of which version you use, the next steps remain the same.

1. Open the Camera app and tap the "chevron" arrow icon at the top of the screen. This action displays additional options at the bottom, just above the shutter icon.

2. You will notice a variety of camera functions, including the extreme filter icon on the right side of the timer mode. Just touch the circle's icon to continue.

3. You now have access to the same filter set as your older iPhones. Just select what you want and take the photo as you wish; this is all there is; the filters you've always known and loved are here to stay, except that some additional steps are required to access them.

Adding filters to your photos is a quick and easy way to improve them, note that there are various tips and tricks you can use to improve your iPhone photography skills.

This change to filter access can be confusing or even a little annoying, especially if you're from one of the older iPhones. However, this is not the only function that has been moved to another section of the camera application. Several existing functions, such as Live Photo, Timer Mode, format change, and more, have been moved to the Camera app and are now all behind the small arrow icon on the Camera app screen.

By the way, you can now also add filters to videos on iPhone and iPad. So if you are a fan of filters, you can also take advantage of this feature.

Camera Test

In shooting bokeh simulation mode, the new iPhone can take good results, but it is not the best. Slight depth estimation errors can be seen in all cases, but the noise on the subject and background has been improved compared to the XS Max. Bokeh mode works well, but it's not the best we've ever seen. This iPhone has one of the best night modes ever examined.

The iPhone 11 Pro Max is equipped with a 2x telephoto lens. Apple has improved the quality of the zoom image, and it works very well at close range, but it is not as good as a phone equipped with a telephoto lens (such as the Huawei Mate 30 Pro or P30 Pro). When shooting at mid-range, the difference It becomes more obvious: when you zoom the lens closer to the subject, the image details become less, and the noise becomes quite large in all cases, the iPhone 11 Pro Max is the first iPhone with an ultra-wide-angle lens, providing one of the widest viewing angles we have ever seen (the actual measured focal length of the viewing angle is 13.7 mm). But it is still much worse than the primary camera, just like almost all mobile phones. The Apple ultra-wide-angle camera has excellent color rendering and good dynamic range; the texture of its ultra-wide-angle image is also more in place than some competing products, but in comparison, it has more noise. Face distortion becomes noticeable near the edges of the screen, but is well controlled, especially when considering its wide field of view.

The new iPhone performed well under a new night photography test benchmark. It performed best when the flash was turned on or off and in night mode; however, the auto flash mode did not work well, and portrait photos were overexposed. The details are not up to standard.

CHAPTER FIVE

The Triple Rear Camera Lens

The triple-lens rear camera, the first for any iPhone, is only found in the iPhone 11 and pro max devices, in this guide we will be talking mainly on the iPhone 11 Pro-Max triple-lens rear cameras. The triple rear camera includes a telephoto and wide-angle lenses along with a new ultra-wide-angle camera lens. All the three lenses are 12-megapixels, and the differences between each of them are explained below;

The Ultra wide-angle camera

- ❖ 12-megapixel sensor
- ❖ 13mm focal length
- ❖ 120-degree field of view

❖ 5-element lens

❖ f/2.4 aperture

❖ This Lens is located at the rightmost

The Wide-Angle camera

❖ The 12-megapixel sensor, allowing more light

❖ The pixels are a hundred percent more focused

❖ Optical image stabilization

❖ f/1.8 aperture

❖ 6-element lens

❖ It's located at the top left

The Telephoto Camera

❖ 12 megapixel

❖ Zoom 2x

❖ 6-element lens

❖ Aperture is f/2.0

- ❖ It captures 40 percent more light than the iPhone XS

- ❖ Optical image stabilization

- ❖ The bottom left lens on the iPhone 11 pro-max is the telephoto camera.

With the ultra-wide-angle lens, iPhone 11 Pro-Max users can now get up to 4times more scenes; this is way better for group portraits, landscape images, and architecture images.

Apple recommends that you use the ultra-wide angle lens for an **artful perspective** when taking a very near shot because it gives incredible unique angles; this is because the focal length is a short one.

When you use the three cameras, it allows you to zoom through the telephoto entering the ultra-wide-angle lens, which zooms 4x more, which are two-timed optical zoom and two-times optical zoom out with a digital zoom up, which is up to 10x.

The new camera interface in the iPhone 11 Pro-Max now displays the entire field of view captured by the ultra-wide-angle lens, notwithstanding when you're taking a telephoto or standard wide-angle shot.

It's designed to allow you to see how a photo is like if zoomed out, which you can do with a tap.

A dedicated button is located in the camera interface; that button is used to change the three camera lenses at will and also improving their focal lengths; this allows you to capture the perfect image.

You can swap between the three camera lenses available no matter what you're doing in the camera app; various camera controls allow you do that.

Apple, however, calibrated each camera individually for white balance, exposure, and other metrics, this is done to make the three-camera work together and function as one. The triple rear camera lens is bonded and calibrated for the module to module alignment; these calibrations are applied to all images in real-time.

According to apple, capturing an image is like taking raw photos from the triple-lens and processing them for a consistent look and color; this calculation happens in splits seconds. This process makes your photo looks the same when you take them using the different camera lenses.

Amazingly, the new HDR feature has been introduced in the iPhone 11 pro-max, it uses high algorithms so it can give out shadow and highlight details in photos. Machine learning feature can know faces in pictures, brilliantly re-editing them for perfect detail for the background and subject.

How to Select Camera Aspect Ratio on Your Device

Apple redesigned the camera app in the iPhone 11 pro-max, and one of the newly updated features is the introduction of different aspect shooting ratio. On earlier versions of the iPhone, the camera app only uses a 1:1 aspect ratio shooting mode, which is called square; if you own the previous version, only select another type of aspect ratio in the editing mode of the photos app.

However, in the iPhone 11 pro-max, owners can select any of the three aspect ratios when snapping photos from the camera: 1:1, 4:3, and 16:9. Follow the steps below to use any aspect ratio;

1. Open the Camera app, then tap the arrow at the top of the viewfinder
2. Select the 4: 3 button in the toolbox that appears directly below the viewfinder
3. Select the desired aspect ratio from the expanded 4: 3 menu
4. Proceed to capture an image.

(**NB**: 1:1 and 16:9 aspect shooting ratio can be re-cropped in the editing window if you have a change of mind in returning to the 4:3 typical frame.)

How to Take Photos with Night Mode Features

Night Mode is a new feature that, when exclusive to the iPhone 11 series, when using the iPhone 11 Pro-Max Camera App, the Night Mode feature automatically turns on when it's dark enough to illuminate an indoor or outdoor scene that leads to a natural reduction in color and noise.

IPhone 11 Pro users will see an immediate improvement in low-light shooting without adjusting exposure settings.

If you want to use night mode, the night mode button that resembles the crescent moon appears at the top of the viewer. If you think the moment will benefit the night mode, press the button. It turns yellow, and the number of seconds for the exposure is displayed.

When night mode is activated, a slider appears under the menu. You can leave it at the suggested exposure or use it manually. More prolonged exposure of 1, 2, or 3 seconds is automatically simulated in night mode. However, depending on the ambient light, you can change the exposure to less than 10 seconds at any time.

To take a photo, click the shutter button and make sure your phone is quiet while the camera simulates long exposure. When the process is complete, you should leave an image that looks like the camera can see dark; however, if you do not want to use the night mode function in low light, tap it when the yellow night mode button appears at the top of the viewfinder to turn it off.

How to Take Burst Photos

First, you may want to know what burst mode is. BURST MODE is when your iPhone's camera creates a series of images in a fast sequence, at a 10-frame per second rate. It's the best way to take an action scene or a stunning photo.

According to Apple, the company has redesigned the BURST MODE mode on iPhone 11 pro-max; in previous versions of the iPhone, the user could hold the capture button for the duration of the scene you are trying to capture.

On the iPhone 11 pro-max, however, you have to tap the shutter button and drag it to the square with the last image you created. The shooter extends elastically under your finger as you perform the function.

See image below

You will notice that the counter increases in the shutter's central position for as long as you hold it down; this shows how many shots are being taken in the current burst, to end to a burst of shots, take your hand off the shutter.

After taking your burst photos, they will automatically save in the Photos app under the album named BURSTS. However, you will also find them in your main photo library.

How to Switch Focal Length

The portrait mode had become a fantastic way of taking impressive shots using a depth of field effect known as BOKEH, allowing iPhone users to shoot an image that keeps the subject real sharp while creating a beautifully blurred background.

Now, using the iPhone 11 Pro-Max, you can change the focal length in portrait mode, thanks to a triple lensed camera system, focal length switching allows for the best shot for the selected scene.

To use portrait mode and move to the focal length, do the following.

1. Launch the Camera app and push the Portrait mode button
2. The portrait lighting effect should appear at the bottom of the viewfinder
3. To change the focal lengths tap the circular 1x button right in the bottom left of the viewfinder

(NB: 1x represents the wide lens, while 2x switches to the telephoto lens)

See image below

The differences between the two modes can be noticed in the second and third images above. Nevertheless, it is said that the 2x mode is best in shooting or capturing people, while the 1x mode is suitable for capturing objects.

CHAPTER SIX

Portrait Mode

The portrait mode usually is an old feature of the iPhone series, however in the iPhone 11 Pro-Max device the portrait mode has been enhanced due to the triple rear camera lens, photos can now be taken with the telephoto lens, wide-angle lens or the ultra-wide-angle lens, which is used for depth perception.

Portrait mode in the iPhone 11 Pro-Max allows images that are focused on a subject in the foreground while the background is blurred.

In the iPhone 11 Pro-Max device, you can make use of the portrait mode to take shots that are zoomed out and also have a full view than before.

The iPhone 11 Pro-Max permits for portrait lighting, which makes for the lighting effects of an image to be shifted while making use of the software. There are several lighting options you can select from, some of which are; Natural, Studio, Contour, Single, monochrome, and multi-purpose.

Follow these simple steps to create a painting.

- ➢ Open your app server
- ➢ Choose the model
- ➢ Call the tips on the page to move your topic to the yellow security line
- ➢ Click the box like the image to select the light effect

- Natural light: this helps the eye to resist the blurred image.
- Flashlight: this one illuminates the screen face, and the image is viewed on the whole
- Lighting: Provides face-to-face features with high lighting and lighting conditions
- Flashlight: this one illuminates the screen in a deeper layer
- *Stage Light Mono:* This effect is similar to stage light, but the images are in black and white.
- *High-key Light Mono:* It effectively creates a grayscale subject on a white background.

1. Tap the red circle to take the shot.

See image below

You can adjust portrait lighting effects in portrait mode, virtually change the position and power of each portrait lighting effect to make the eyes more visible with a smooth face.

To adjust the portrait lighting effect in portrait mode follow these steps;

1. Select portrait mode, then frame your subject
2. Tap the hexagon-like icon on the screen top. (This allows the portrait lighting slider to pop up below the frame).

3. Drag the slider to either right or left to adjust the effect to your satisfaction

4. Tap the red circle to take the shot

You can as well adjust the depth control in portrait mode; this allows you to make any adjustment for the blur in your portrait mode images.

To adjust depth control in portrait mode, follow these simple steps below:

1. Open your camera app
2. Select portrait mode, then frame your subject
3. Tap the circle with letter f in it at the top right part of the screen (The depth control slider appears below the frame).

4. Drag the slider to either right or left to adjust the effect to your satisfaction

5. Tap the red or white circle to take the shot.

See image below

How to Use Quick Take

Apple has now changed the way you shoot videos in its new series, on an older or earlier version of iPhone you had to select a video from below the viewfinder, but now apple as implemented the new "quick take" feature.

Using iPhone 11 Pro-Max, you can record videos even without switching from the current photo mode, record videos, tap and hold the red shutter button, then release it to stop recording.

To keep videoing without having to press down the button, slide the circle button to the right, the circle will stretch in between your finger as you do so, and a target padlock icon will appear.

See image below

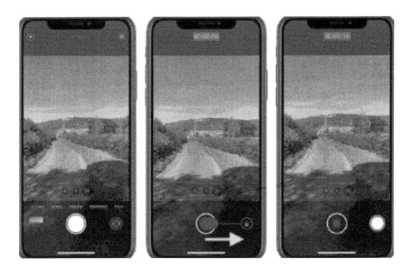

Once the padlock is placed, the shutter button will remain located there for as long as you record the video. Amazingly, you can still tap the shutter to take a still photo during the video recording, when you are ready to end the video recording; tap the record button below the viewfinder.

Other Camera Features

The iPhone 11 Pro-Max camera features are extensive; there's a different dedicated guide that talks about iPhone 11 Pro-Max camera features and everything about it. However, there are some other features we need to touch; some of them include; Thirty-six percent lighter True tone flashlight, Sixty Three Megapixel panoramas which could be 2x high, wide color shot, live photos support, burst mood, and advanced red-eye correction.

In iOS 13.2, Apple introduced a feature known as deep fusion; it is a new image processing system that uses a neural engine and an A13 Bionic. This deep fusion uses advanced machine learning techniques, which do pixel by pixel processing of photos.

This deep fusion is aimed at enhancing indoor and mid-level photos. The function is automatically activated based on the level of lenses and room lighting used, not something that is possible.

Video capabilities

According to Apple, the iPhone 11 Pro-Max offers high-definition video on any smartphone, camera, wide-angle lens, and ultra-wide angle lenses work in video mode, and you can turn them on while recording.

The iPhone 11 Pro-Max camcorder captures 4k video at 60 frames per second with both lenses, and the ultra-wide camera can also capture up to four times more scenes for better action shots.

The iPhone 11 pro-max supports extended dynamic range when recording videos at 60 frames per second. Optical image stabilization is also available for video recording using a standard wide-angle camera.

The purpose of the Audio Zoom feature is to match the audio in the video, so you get better sound when recording video from the iPhone 11 pro-max.

Animoji and Memoji

The new True Depth camera system supports two main functions, Animoji and Memoji. These features are animated, 3D emoticon characters that you can control with your face. Animoji emoticons are style creatures, while Memoji is customizable, personalized avatars that you can create and manipulate.

To enable Animoji and Memoji True-Depth camera analyzes more than 50 muscle movements in different areas of the face, detecting eyebrows, jaws, jaws, eyes, jaws, mouths, opposing movements, and mouth. All your facial movements will be translated to the Animoji/Memoji characters, which allows them, reflect your emotion and expression.

You can share Animoji and Memoji with friends and also use it in social media chats and messages as well as FaceTime apps.

There are hundreds of Animoji to choose from, modeled after existing emoji characters: mouse, octopus, warthog, lion, poop, fox, robot, chicken, alien, unicorn, giraffe, owl, shark, bear and tiger to mention a few.

There are also unlimited memoji characters that can be made to look like you and others.

True-Depth Camera ID and Face ID

iPhone 11 Pro-Max has had the face ID feature; it is called a biometric facial identification system used by Apple since 2017. The facial identification faces are housed in the True Depth camera system on the front of the iPhone.

The new iPhone 11 Pro-Max has introduced an updated, True Depth camera system that uses new hardware. Now it's 30 percent faster on unlocking devices and passwords and authentication purchases, in addition to being designed from a wide range of angles.

Face ID is used across iOS for unlocking you're the device; it can also be used to allow access to third party pass codes-protected apps, confirming iTunes payments and the App store Purchases, it, however, authenticates apple pay payments.

The Face ID works through a set of sensors and cameras that are in-built in the True Depth camera system of the iPhone 11 pro-max. You can create a 3D facial scan that would correctly map the curves and planes of any face; a Dot Projector projects more than 30,000 invisible infrared dots onto the surface of the skin, which will be read by an infrared camera. The depth map is then sent to the bionic processor A13, where it is transformed into a mathematical model used by the iPhone that you want to find on your device.

An infrared ID, which allows it to function better in low light conditions and even in the dark, has a floodlighting in place, which ensures that there is always sufficient light to face a scan. Identity recognition can work with beards, hats, glasses, scarves, makeup, and even sunglasses and all accessories and other objects that meet many faces; the only thing it needs to see is your eyes, nose, and mouth, with this it would perform its work.

A13 Bionic chip and the Neural engine helps the face ID adjust to minor facial changes over time; that is to say, if however you grow a beard or your hair becomes more protracted, face ID will adapt and continue to unlock your iPhone 11 pro-max.

Camera Controls and Tips

1. Turn the dark mode on iOS 13

You love the new dark mode on iOS 13. It immediately changes the color scheme and provides a natural background with text, it helps with battery life, and it is beneficial for the eyes.

To change the dark mode, open the Control Center, and join the Bright bar. In the lower-left, you will see a new change of dark mode. Tap to change it to dark mode.

2. Learn about touch

Apple has the 3D Touch element to use the new iPhone 11 Pro series; this means that you only keep an object with a contextual menu. Previously, you had to press harder on the screen; this means that there is a new way to reset applications. And previews operate differently in safari. But overall, this is a significant change. Just contact an app menu, link, or icon for more information.

3. Go to a wide camera

Tap the 0.5x button to switch to the ultra-wide sensor quickly.

4. Go to telephoto lens

Tap the 2x button to change the telephoto lens; this provides a 2x optical zoom level.

5. Use the zoom level between 0.5x and 2x

While the level buttons provide accurate zoom, you can use a zoom level between 0.5x and 2x. These cameras vary entirely in the background. Just slide the zoom buttons to reveal them and dial. Swim to change the zoom level. 8. Record video in 4K from any rear sensor

Go to Settings -> Camera -> Video Recording and switch to 4K. Please note that although you can record 4K videos from any rear camera, it is limited to 30 frames per second. At 60 frames per second, you cannot switch between three camera sensors when recording video.

6. Record a 4K Video from the Selfie Camera

On the same settings screen, you can also change the resolution for the front camera to 4K.

7. Take Slo-fie

Switch to the front camera and swipe to the new Slo-mo option to start recording slow-motion video from the front camera. Or, as Apple calls it, stupid. 11. Zoom out on an ultra-wide camera while editing

When you take photos, iPhone 11 takes pictures of the wide and ultra-wide sensors. And it takes extremely wide photographs for a while; this allows you to enter the edit screen and zoom out so you can add ultra-wide photos later.

8. Use the Night mode

Apple is finally in night mode on the iPhone camera, and better than the Pixel 3.

Although the Pixel 3 takes flamboyant night-time shots, it does compromise on detail. The iPhone 11, in the typical iPhone style, captures natural-looking night shots filled with detail, even at night.

The night mode function operates automatically, and there is no button on the user interface. It turns on automatically when the Camera app detects low light conditions.

Although night mode is excellent, it does not work with ultra-wide sensors.

9. Use the New QuickTake feature

It is a new feature in the Camera app, shipped within a few weeks of the release of the iPhone 11.

Now you can touch and hold the shutter button to instantly start recording video, much like it works on Snapchat. The video stays in the same frame and takes photos as photos, which is very impressive.

If you continue to record video for a long time, you can slide it to the right to shut it to video recording mode. 14. Take photos taken

To shoot in Burst mode, touch the shutter button and drag it to the left.

10. Change the intensity of the filter

When you start in a photo editing mode, you can now adjust the brightness of the filter after selecting a new filter.

11. Cut and rotate 4K video

Tap the Edit Video button to find new ways to rotate or crop the video you've recorded quickly. You can also use photo editing touches like changing exposure and more.

12. Use the New Gestures of Text Gestures

Apple also takes text choices seriously. Now you can touch and hold the cursor to lift it and move it immediately.

Selecting text is much more comfortable. Just touch a word and drag it to the desired point, for example, at the end of the paragraph. IOS selects all the text between the colon.

After selecting the text, you can copy it with gestures. Just pinch it with three fingers to copy it, tweak it with three fingers to glue it, and pull it back with three fingers to cancel typing or action. Use the face ID from a different angle.

iPhone 11 series Face ID, is quite fast, and it works from a wider angle. So, even if your iPhone is not in front of you, Face ID will now unlock your phone for you.

13. Try to write a gesture

The iPhone 11 Pro comes with a significant upgrade of the keyboard. Now you can slide your finger over the letters on the keyboard to form words; this is similar to how SwiftKey and Gboard work.

14. Get the Main Back Button

If you have an iPhone 7 or iPhone 8, you may lose the Home button. Although you can't reset the actual Home button, there is an option to use the Home button on the iPhone 11 pro max using its 'Accessibility feature,' Go to the settings -> General -> Accessibility -> Assisted Contact and enter shortcuts for single-touch keys, double-tap, long-press, and 3D touch for the Assisted Help button. With one touch, arrange to go home. By defining other gesture features, you can use features that you find challenging to find.

15. Purchase of lighting headphones

Maybe you have already noticed that your new iPhone was shiny without Lighting and a 3.5mm headphones adapter. Apple has packed new iPhones from iPhone 7, but not so now. If you have already purchased AirPod, or otherwise use Apple EarPod, you may not need the adapter.

However, for the majority of people, it is good to be in the back. You may need it in your car or when we connect speakers to your friend's house.

16. Take pictures in RAW format

The iPhone 11 Pro takes excellent photos with the new HDR Smart method. You can also use an application like Halide to capture raw images with manual controls. You can set exposure, focus, brightness, and more. The app also has a first depth mode.

17. Take better pictures

You have received photos from Smart HDR mode or Halide; they are pretty good, but you can make them even better by using the photo editing feature. Snapseed and Darkroom are the best choices for us. Both are intuitive to use. In the darkroom, you can choose from a fantastic collection of filters.

Zoom

The iPhone 11 Pro Max is equipped with a 2x optical telephoto lens, which can provide a field of view equivalent to 52 mm. In this configuration, the Apple phone can shoot good results under close-range zoom, and the image quality is better than XS Max, but its performance in the mid-to-long distance is still not as good as that of some competitors and 5x lenses. The noise of the iPhone's zoom image can be seen in all light conditions, but the phone scored the highest score in a camera equipped with a 2x lens.

The Apple phone's zoom can capture details in close range (2x), and its performance is almost equal to that of the Mate 30 Pro equipped with a 3x telephoto lens.

Bokeh

Apple iPhone 11 Pro Max has achieved excellent results in the bokeh project, which is a slight improvement over the XS Max; this is mainly because the phone has less noise, but still does not reach the level of the best competing products. The portrait mode images show good depth estimation, beautiful bokeh shapes, and gradient levels, making the overall effect look very natural.

Night Photography

The iPhone 11 Pro Max's total night photography score is 53 points, and its performance does not vary from the best phones tested; it is also one of the best performing phones when the flash is off. Its images show good exposure, natural white balance, and color rendering, even in tricky mixed lighting conditions, and the skin tones of people in portraits are perfect. The disadvantage is that we saw some spill clipping textures in the illuminated areas of the scene, and some slight ghosting also appeared on the moving subject.

On the other hand, there is still room for improvement in the auto flash mode. In this mode, the camera can capture pretty good details, but the noise is apparent, and the flash occasionally triggers when shooting landscape photos, but it can't illuminate the entire scene. We also saw some overexposure of the faces in the portrait photos, which caused the skin to have a light cut texture and incorrect color rendering.

However, in the case of forcibly turning on the flash, the performance of the camera is not bad, and it is significantly improved than the XS Max. In total darkness and feeble ambient light, the white balance and exposure are accurate, but the edges of the image show some noticeable flash drops. When shooting at 0 lux, our testers also observed some slight exposure changes in a series of continuous photos.

The night mode on Apple is one of the best modes seen so far, second only to Google's Night Sight mode. In some cases, the iPhone 11 Pro Max's night mode can get better image quality than the standard flash off mode, so it was added a bit in the night photography test. The color rendering of night mode is usually pleasing, with less noise than photos taken at the default settings. However, if the camera detects a person's face, it appears to apply another image processing to outline the facial details.

CHAPTER SEVEN

Battery Life

The iPhone 11 Pro-Max has improved battery life thanks to a combination of A13 Bionic panels and improvements to the ultra-retained XDR display and new Apple-designed power management units.

The battery life of the iPhone 11 Pro-Max is five hours longer than the iPhone XS when it comes to actual use, the iPhone 11 Pro-Max can last up to 20 hours when playing a video file, or up to 80 hours when playing audio juice. The iPhone 11 Pro-Max battery is thicker and heavier than the XS and XS max. The iPhone 11 Pro-Max has a maximum battery life of 3969 mAh, which is higher than the iPhone 11 with a 3.046 mAh battery. The

Dark-mode feature not only allows you to enjoy your device without disturbing others but also offers energy-saving benefits.

Fast Charging Feature

The iPhone 11 Pro-Max has a fast charge function that can be loaded from a dead-end to 50% of the charge in just 30 minutes using a higher power charger. According to Apple, they include the hardware required for fast charging, so the iPhone 11 Pro-Max charges faster than ever. The iPhone 11 Pro-Maxis comes with an 18 W USB-C power adapter.

Wireless Charging

The glass body of the iPhone 11 Pro-Max has a built-in wireless charging coil that supports wireless charging.

Apple said the iPhone 11 Pro-Max uses Qi wireless charging, and most high-end Android devices also offer this feature, which also means that the new iPhone 11 Pro-Max can use any Qi-certified inductive charger for wireless charging.

The iPhone 11 Pro-Max can also use 7.5 W and 5 W wireless charging accessories, but the 7.5 W charging speed is faster. However, some 7.5W The iPhone 11 pro-max charger is no longer charging at 5W, and it's worth noting if you decide to buy a wireless charger.

Charging and Monitoring Your Battery

Most iPhones come with a built-in rechargeable lithium-ion battery for the best performance for your device. Lithium-ion batteries are lighter, charge faster, last longer, and have higher battery densities for longer battery life.

Follow these steps to charge the battery:

- Connect the iPhone 11 Pro-Max to a power source with the included flash speed with a USB cable and USB power adapter.
- You can also charge your iPhone 11 Pro-Max by connecting your computer with a USB cable
- Charge your iPhone 11 Pro-Max wirelessly by placing it on a QI-certified charger

Charging and operating your device at the same time can result in a slow charging experience. When the iPhone is low, it shows an image of a drained battery, indicating that it needs to be charged up to 10 minutes before use.

If you find that there is liquid in the iPhone flash unit, do not use it to charge the iPhone, wait for it to dry, or use only a wireless charger or other connectors.

Using LOW POWER MODE can significantly increase the life of battery charge, you can switch to LOW POWER MODE when your battery is low or when you do not have access to electricity.

Launch your SETTINGS APP and Tap the BATTERY, then turn on LOW POWER MODE.

(**NB:** if your iPhone switches to low power mode automatically it switches back to normal power mode after charging to 80%, note that your iPhone may perform some tasks slowly in low power mode)

CHAPTER EIGHT

All Applications

Applications are the significant features in any smart device; they are what the device is made up of, they are what it uses to perform its duties, apps are inbuilt and are also external, in this chapter we will be explaining some of the in-built apps found in iPhone 11 Pro-Max device.

However, you can switch between apps using the minimize and maximize features; you can also group and organize your apps and as well remove them.

Some of the apps we will be talking about are listed below:

1. **App Store:** Apple app store is an online store exclusive to Apple devices; in this store, you can get games, get other apps, download fonts, keyboards, and subscribe. Some apps can only be purchased, whereby you will have to use apple pay.

2. **Books:** This is an app you use to find and explore books of your choice, including audiobooks, PDFs, and ebooks. You can organize your books and set your reading goals in the app, and also listen to audiobooks.

3. **Calendar:** We all know what the calendar app is used for. However, there are some other features it can do; you could create events and as well edit them, you can send and receive invitations, you can search for events, keep track of events and share iCloud calendars.

4. **Camera:** We have discussed everything the camera app can do in previous chapters, the camera in the iPhone 11 Pro-Max has been fully enhanced to suit any photo-lover tastes.

5. **Itunes Store:** This is an app that is exclusive to iOS devices; with iTunes stores, you can get the latest music online, movies, and even TV shows; you can also purchase movies and music.

6. **News:** With this app, you can get started with news daily, view news stories, and see new stories chosen just for you.

7. **Apple news:** This is an app exclusive to iOS devices; with this app, you can browse and read apple news+ stories and happenings, subscribe to apple news, search for new

stories, save the news for later and subscribe to news.

8. **Notes:** In this app, you can put down notes during seminars, lectures, or any program; the notes app allows drawing or use handwriting, add attachments. You can also search and organize your notes, share and collaborate, lock notes, and change settings.

9. **Voice Memos:** With this app, you can record voice notes and play it back; you could edit or delete a recording, share a recording, and also duplicate a recording.

10. **Music:** This is a simple app for everyone; it is used to play music, listen to broadcast radio, and view albums.

These are some of the in-built apps of the iPhone 11 pro-max; we cannot mention and explain all the apps in this guide. However, you will come to know all the apps as you explore your new device.

EXPLORING THE HOME SCREEN

You will have to get familiar with your home screen and apps. The home screen shows all your apps organized into pages. More pages are automatically added when you need more space for incoming apps.

To get the home screen, swipe up from the bottom of the screen after unlocking with either your face ID or passcodes.

Swipe sideways to see other pages with more apps, to open an app, tap on the icon, to get to the home screen, swipe up from the bottom of the screen.

See image below

How TO Perform a Screenshot

A screenshot means capturing the page you are in that moment, a screenshot helps in saving things you can easily forget. To take a screenshot, do the below;

1. To take a screenshot, press the side button with the Up Volume Up button at the same time

When you save the screenshot, you'll be able to see it later in the screenshot album of the Photos app or all photo albums after launching iCloud Photos.

How to Use the Screen Recorder

The on-screen recording feature lets you record videos of what happened on the screen of your device, useful when you're trying to teach you how to get on the phone, and surprisingly it captures the sound as well. To record a screen, follow the steps below;

1. Open the Settings app, tap Control Center, select the controls as desired, and then tap the green circle next to the screen capture.

2. Open the Control Center, tap the record icon, and then wait for the three-second count.

3. To CANCEL, open the Control Center, tap the red status bar at the top of the screen, and then select Stop.

Go to Photos, then select your screenshot.

How to Change Sounds and Vibrations

You can change the sound and vibration of your iPhone when you receive your call, text message, reminder, email, or any other kind of notification; you can change the sound that is coming.

To set sound and vibration options, follow the steps below;

1. Launch the Settings app, scroll to Sound & Content
2. To manipulate the volume of all sounds, move the slider below the ringtone and alert.
3. When setting the sound and vibration pattern for sound, tap on a type of sounds such as a ringtone or text tone.
4. Do one of the following;
- Select a tone (scroll to see them all)

Ringing tones play incoming calls, clock alarms, and clock counters when text messages are used for text messages, new voice messages, and other notifications alerts

- Tap vibration, choose a vibration pattern, tap 'Create New Vibration' to create your own.

(**NB:** when you are not seeing or hearing incoming calls and alerts when you expect them, open control center, then check if DO NOT DISTURB is on. If the half-crescent moon is highlighted, tap it to turn off DO NOT DISTURB.)

How to Use and Customize the Control Center

The control center gives you instant access to DO NOT DISTURB, A FLASHLIGHT, AIRPLANE MODE, and other handy features.

To open the control center in the pro-max iPhone 11, slide your finger up from the bottom of the screen to swipe down from the top-right edge to close the control center.

Some controls offer additional options in the control center, to see the available options, touch and hold control. Here are some examples below

- Touch and hold the top-left group of control, then tap the hotspot-like icon to open airdrop options.
- Tap and hold the camera icon to take a selfie, take a photo, or even record a video.

See image below

Touch and hold to
see Camera options.

You can temporarily disconnect WIFI and Bluetooth from the control center, but however the WIFI or Bluetooth would not go off, so you may have to go and put them off from the settings app.

You can add and organize your control center, to do this, follow the steps below;

1. Launch Settings app, tap CONTROL CENTER, select CUSTOMIZE CONTROLS
2. To add or remove controls, tap the green circle to add, or you tap the red circle to remove.

3. To rearrange the controls, hold down the three short lines next to the controller, then drag it to a new position.

How to View and Also Organize Today-View

With "Today," you can get information from your favorite apps at a glance, see today's headlines, weather, calendar, events, tips, and more.

To open today, swipe from left to right on the home or lock screen.

You can add and organize your tour today and widgets, follow these steps;

1. Go to "Today," swipe up, then click "Edit" at the bottom of the screen
2. To add or remove widgets, click the green or red button.
3. To rearrange the Today widgets, press and hold three short lines, and then drag it to a new position

See image below

CHAPTER NINE

Accessing Features from a Locked Screen

If the screen is locked, it displays the current time and date and your latest notice. On the lock screen, you see a notification, open the camera and access control center; you can also get information from your favorite applications and much more.

You can easily and quickly access some features and information you need urgently from the locked screen, even when the device is still locked. From the locked screen to do any of the following;

• Open Camera: Swipe to left

• Open Control center: Swipe it from the bottom of the screen

• See earlier notifications: Swipe it from the center

• See today view: Swipe it right

You can set your iPhone 11 Pro-Max to show notifications preview when the screen is locked; notifications preview includes; texts from messages, lines from mails, and details about calendar invitation. To activate the function, follow the steps below;

1. Launch Settings app, tap NOTIFICATIONS

2. Select SHOW PREVIEW, then tap ALWAYS.

How to Set Screen Time Allowances and Limits

Using screen time, you can set allowances and limits for app use, schedule downtime, and more. You can manipulate any of these settings at any time.

You can block apps and notifications during the period you want time away from your device, to perform that function, do the below;

1.	Open the Settings app, select screen

2.	Click on the startup screen, select sold, and then click SO MY IPHONE

3.	Click DOWNTIME, and then turn DOWNTIME

4.	Select each day or set the date, and then set the start and end time

You can also set application limits that is to establish a time limit for a category of applications as well as for individual apps. To perform this function, do the following:

1.   Run Settings, click SCREEN TIME

2.   If you could not turn the screen on time, turn it on, click CONTINUE, and then click THIS IS MY IPHONE

3.   Select the application limits, and then click Add limit

4.   Select one or more categories of applications.

To apply restrictions to individual supplements, click a category name to view all the applications in this category, and then select the app that you want to restrict. (Note: If you choose multiple application categories, the date that you specify will be applied to all of them.)

5.   Click Next, and then set the desired time.

6.   When you're ready to set limits, click ADD, to return to the app restrictions

If you want to disable the application restriction temporarily, click the application of restrictions on the screen the application of restrictions; to eliminate the limitation of the application for a specific category, click the category, and then click on the restriction of the application. If you want to remove the restriction of the categories, click the category, and then click to remove the restriction.

Learn the Meaning of Status Icons

DUAL CELL SIGNALS: The iPhone 11 Pro-Max supports dual sim, the upper row of the bar indicates the line signal, which you use for cellular data, while the lower power signal indicates a different line when there is no signal at all, it does not reflect the service.

Airplane Mode: If airplane mode is enabled, you can make phone calls or surf the Internet, and other wireless communication functions are disabled.

LTE: This means that your carrier for LTE is available, and the iPhone can connect to the Internet through this network

5GE: this indicates that your network is available 5GE, and iPhone can connect to the Internet through this network.

GPRS: GPRS / 1xRTT, which means that your GPRS (GSM) or 1xRTT (CDMA) operator is available, and the iPhone can connect to the Internet through the network.

Go to support.apple.com, to view all icons and their states of use.

Health

Health - is an embedded application for the iPhone 11 pro-max, which helps collect health and fitness data, view health and fitness information, monitor menstrual circles, control audio volume, and more others. You can share your health and fitness data with your family and friends; you can also download health records and as well create a medical ID. Take your time to explore the health app and keep yourself healthy.

Reminders

Using the reminders app, you can easily set up and set up alerts to track each stage of the shot; this can be used in the store, for work, for homework, and whatever else you want to see. You can create subtasks, raise flags, add attachments, and choose where and when to receive reminders. The smart list will also help you automatically adjust your reminder.

To add a reminder, you can ask SIRI, say something like "Add artichokes to mu groceries list" or do the following listed below;

1.   Tap new Reminder, enter text

2.   You can use the quick toolbar above the keyboard to perform any of these;

•   Schedule a date or time: Tap the clock icon, then select a date for a full-day reminder, tap custom to set a date and time for you to be notified.

•   Add a location: Tap the envelope-like icon to choose where you want to be reminded, e.g., when you leave work or get home.

•   Set the flag: Tap the flag to mark the main memory

• Display a photo or list: Launch a camera icon to take a new photo, select an existing image in your photo library, or copy that image.

3. To add content to a notification, tap the blue circle and then do one of the following;

• Add Notes: In the Notes section, provide additional information related to the notification

• Add Website: Under the URL line, enter the website.

• Tell when chatting with someone in the comments: Understand me when messaging and then select someone from your list, when next you talk to that person in the comment, you will be notified.

• Pre-set: Tap the option first, then select the action option

- Tap Done

Shortcuts

When you use the shortcut app, it helps you automate a task you do often with just a tap or by asking SIRI. You can create a shortcut to get directions to the next event in your calendar; you can also move text from one place to another, and more. Select ready-made shortcuts from the gallery or build your own using different apps to run multiple steps in a task.

Using the Car Play Feature

You can connect your iPhone to CarPlay to get directions, make calls, listen to music, check your calendar, and more on the Carplay screen.

However, CarPlay is available only in certain regions, and it is also available on selected models, the CarPlay feature is available in the iPhone 11 pro-max.

To set up CarPlay, you will need to connect your device to your vehicle; you can do this using your vehicle's USB port or its wireless capability.

When trying to connect, ensure that SIRI is enabled, if it is not, launch the Settings app, then tap on SIRI & SEARCH, then turn on:

- Press the side button for SIRI

When you want to connect your iPhone to your vehicle using the USB cable, use only Apple-approved Lightning to USB cable.

The USB area may be marked with a CarPlay icon or a photo of a smartphone.

When using a vehicle that supports wireless connection, Use the following procedures to connect to your car to your iPhone.

1. With a vehicle that supports wireless CarPlay, do one of the following;

• Click and hold the voice command button located on your steering wheel.

• Ensure that your vehicle is in wireless or Bluetooth pairing mode.

2. On your iPhone pro max, launch the Settings app, tap GENERAL, select CARPLAY, then choose AVAILABLE CARS.

3. Choose your vehicle

Some vehicle CarPlay home automatically comes up when you connect your iPhone to it, however, if CarPlay home does not display, select the car play logo on your vehicle's display.

CHAPTER TEN

Photo Rating

Apple iPhone 11 Pro Max has a photo score of 124 points, which ranks among the top ten in photo ranking, and is the same as the Samsung Galaxy S10 5G. After testing the performance of this mobile phone's static image in several aspects under different lighting conditions, we scored each test item and calculated the photo score. In this section, we will carefully study how the scores of these test items come from and compare the image quality of some major competitors.

Color Score

The iPhone's color score is almost the best, thanks to its pleasing color rendering and vibrant color saturation. Also, it can shoot accurate white balance under all lighting conditions. As with previous models, Apple adjusted the color of the camera image to a slightly yellowish color rendering. The effect is not adverse, it is still within the acceptable range, and in most cases, it can shoot good results; this produces a particularly beneficial effect on skin tones in portrait photography. In some indoor and laboratory images, we have observed a slightly greenish color cast, but overall, the color of the 11 Pro Max is significantly improved than the XS Max, because the latter has more color cast and is less stable.

The phone also performs very similarly in indoor conditions. Likewise, Apple and Samsung images are still very close, but the saturation of the Note 10+ 5G images is slightly higher and slightly more accurate. The overall color is arguably the best of these contrast proofs. Huawei images are still cold, and the saturation is marginally lower than other photos.

Camera Noise

Apple phones have always been noisy the same as their latest model. The iPhone 11 Pro Max image processing mainly focuses on details rather than noise reduction; under all lighting conditions, the noise will appear in the stable color area, but this situation has been improved compared to the iPhone XS Max. Its brightness noise particles are more elegant and smaller than the coarse noise we see on some other phones is much better.

There is also some noise in the low-light photos below. However, considering this low-light situation, the performance of the iPhone 11 Pro Max is not bad, but the Mate 30 Pro shoots better details and less noise; the Note 10+ 5G image also lacks details, and a lot of sharpness appears, but noise is managed.

Video Autofocus

Video autofocus is very smooth, has a useful tracking function, and the anti-shake system can play a perfect role in most cases. Only when you walk and shoot, you will see the jitter effect in the iPhone video. Apple iPhone 11 Pro Max's autofocus has performed very well in a laboratory test and real-world shooting. It is swift, can accurately lock the focus in all light conditions, and the repeatability of the focus results is very high.

Video Mode

When you switch the camera to video mode, the iPhone 11 Pro Max can record some of the best movies we've seen on smartphones, especially when using 4K resolution. The phone won the highest video score (102 points), and only Xiaomi CC9 Pro Exclusive Edition performed as well as it did.

The iPhone is one of the few phones that can record HDR movies. It produces a vast dynamic range, and in most cases, the exposure is usually good. The color rendering is quite pleasing and very similar to still images, but the white balance may be somewhat unstable when recording indoors. The 11 Pro Max records excellent details at 4K resolution, and noise is well controlled in highlights.

Video Rating Description

Apple iPhone 11 Pro Max has an overall video score of 102 points and is ranked as the best video phone along with Xiaomi CC9 Premier Edition. Like the photo score, the whole video score comes from the phone's performance and achievements in the following test items: exposure (90), color (90), autofocus (93), texture (75), noise (79), artifacts (85), and Optical image stabilization (94).

In the default settings, the iPhone 11 Pro Max records video at 30 frames per second at 1080p Full HD resolution, but it obtained the best recording results at 4K resolution. Those who frequently switch between video resolution or frame rate will be pleased to see Apple make this process very easy. During recording, click a button to switch between different video frame rates and resolutions. When switching between different frame rates or resolutions, the preview image on display briefly becomes blurred.

Video films often exhibit good exposure, and video HDR gives the film a very wide dynamic range, capturing excellent details in the highlights and shadows of the frame. However, we have also observed some issues with instability in tone mapping, which can cause slight flickering effects in the sky, clouds, or reflective surfaces. In shallow light, its exposure brightness is not as good as the phone that performed best in this test item.

Video Noise

The phone's overall score is close to the Galaxy Note 10+ 5G (42 points), but, just like its primary camera, these two phones use different compromises between texture and noise. Apple images present more luxurious details than Samsung images, but usually noisier, its color rendering is exquisite, and the deformation problem (face deformation) can be seen near the edge of the picture, but in consideration of the wide-field view of the lens, this deformation problem can also be regarded as excellent control.

This Apple camera has achieved outstanding results in bokeh projects. Just like still photos, its color rendering is warm and pleasant, but the white balance may sometimes be unstable, and it changes too fast under varying lighting conditions. Noise also appears when recording in low light and typical indoor conditions, but noise is well controlled in high light, which is roughly comparable to the performance of competing products. When shooting in 4K mode, the camera will record rich details in high light and indoors, but the details will become less in low light.

Video Stabilization

The iPhone 11 Pro Max has excellent video stabilization, but its score in this test project is slightly lower than the previous generation XS Max, mainly because the jitter effect is more obvious. When shooting while walking, the trees, buildings, and other objects near the edge of the picture will be a little deformed, but the problem of deformation can be better controlled in the center of the image. In general, Apple has done an outstanding job of video stabilization.

CHAPTER ELEVEN

How to Record and Edit Slow Motion Video on iPhone 11 Pro Max

1. Launch the camera app on your iPhone.

❖ Activate the front-facing camera by tapping the perspective button below the viewfinder.

❖ In the shooting mode options, swipe just below the viewfinder until the slow-motion is set-off in yellow.

1. Tap the red shutter button to record slow-motion and tap again to finish.

1. To show Slofie, select it in the Photos app, and it will play automatically. If necessary, you can share immediately by clicking the Share button (rectangle with an arrow) and choosing one of several options on the sharing sheet.

How to Adjust Slo-Mo Settings on iPhone 11 Pro Max

Want to use the Slo-Mo features of your iPhone? Follow the instructions to change the settings from the default slow video speed. The latest iPhone models have slow motion at 120 or 240 frames per second at 720p or 1080p.

1. Open the settings

3. Swipe down and tap Camera

11.   Touch Record Slo-Mo video

4. Select 1080p HD at 120 or 240 fps

How to turn Slow Motion Clip into a Regular Video

You can also remove the effects of slow-motion video and effectively restore the video to average speed with the same video editing tool that is maintained in slow motion:

- If you have not done it, open the Photos' app and tap the slow-motion video that you want to convert to an average speed

- Click on the 'Edit' button

1. Click Edit to edit the slow-motion video

- Use two small sliders on the slow-motion timeline to shrink a portion of the slow-motion timeline until it connects to one, removing any slow motion from the video.

1. Tap "Done" to save your changes and convert the video to normal speed

How to Change Normal Video to Slow Motion

Select video mode.

•Touch the record button or press any volume button to start recording.

•To take the photo, press the white shutter button.

•Pin the screen to zoom in and out. To zoom in on iPhone 11 Pro Max, touch and hold 1x and then drag the slider to the left. Tap 0.5 to minimize.

•Touch the record button or press any volume button to stop recording.

By default, videos are recorded at 30 fps (frames per second). You can make other settings for frame rate and video resolution under Settings> Camera> Record video, the faster the rate of the frame, the higher the resolution, the higher the resulting video file.

How to Speed up or slow down a Slow Motion Video

You can change the speed of each clip in the iMovie. Also, iMovie can automatically adjust the frame rate of each clip to match the frame rate of the video (determined by the first clip you add to the video).

- Rabbit symbols and speed controls appear on clips in the timeline

- Change clip speed

- In the timeline, select the clip whose speed you want to change.

- To display the speed controls, click the Speed button.

Speed button in the settings bar

- Choose Slow or Fast from the Speed pop-up menu, and click the speed button to set the speed.

7. Speed control appears above clip in the viewer

Note: If you select Fast for clips shorter than 0.1 seconds, the Custom Speed option will be applied, and you can enter a custom speed.

1. An icon (turtle or rabbit) appears in the clip, and the speed control appears at the top.

- Turtle symbols and speed controls appear on clips in the timeline

❖ Slower clips become longer in the timeline, while accelerated clips become shorter.

Note: If the clip contains audio, playing the clip slowly decreases the pitch, and playing the clip faster increases the pitch. To maintain the original pitch of the audio, select the "Preserve pitch" checkbox above the viewer.

Change clip speed adjustment

- In the timeline, drag the speed slider to the top of the clip, whose speed changes.

- Rabbit symbols and speed controls appear on clips in the timeline

- ❖ Dragging the slider to the right will reduce the speed of the clip, and dragging the slider to the left will speed up the clip. Using the speed slider is useful for custom speed adjustments, as you will see the duration of the clip change in the timeline as you drag the slider.

Change the speed of clip parts

- Each part of the clip can be speeded up or slowed down, and you can choose to change the frame rate smoothly between the region where the speed changes and the rest of the clip.

- Hold down the R key and drag over the clip to select a region in the clip in the timeline.

➢ To display the speed controls, click the Speed button.

Speed button in the settings bar

Do one of the following:

- Slow down selected portions of the clip: Click the Speed pop-up menu, then choose Slow Down.

1. The speed is set to 50% by default, but you can click any speed button.

1. Speed up selected parts of a clip: Click the Speed pop-up menu, then choose Fast.

❖ By default, the speed is set to twice the average rate (2x), but you can click any speed button.

- Set a custom speed for a selected portion of the clip: Click the Speed pop-up menu, choose Custom, and then type a number in the box.

- The speed change is applied to the selected area, and the speed control appears above the chosen area and all areas of the clip outside the area you want.

Speed-dependent clips for region selection

- ❖ When the clip plays, it starts at the average speed, changes to the speed you set, and then returns to the average speed when the clip ends.

- Select the Smooth checkbox to change the speed gradually.

1. Drag the three-speed controls at the top of the clip, adjust the selected area or outside area of the speed.

4. Turtle symbol and speed control displayed in clips in the timeline

Play clip backward

1. Select the clip in the timeline.

4. To display the speed controls, click the Speed button.

Speed button in the settings bar

6. Select the Reverse checkbox.

1. A reverse playback icon will appear on the clip, and the clip will now play backward at the speed you set.

Reverse play icon on clip in the timeline

6. Slow the clip at a high frame rate to make it faster

How to Shoot Cinematic Video on iPhone 11 Pro Max

Do you wonder why every time you shoot on your iPhone it comes out looking like it was shot on an iPhone? So I believe you want to learn how to make your footage look as cinematic and filmy as possible. Here I will share with you three tricks that helped my iPhone start acting like a cinema camera and trust me when your phone behaves like a cinema camera you will be able to get high-quality footage. The reason why your iPhone content isn't looking cinematic is that you are shooting it with the wrong shutter speed or in the wrong frame rate. Like I mentioned before I'm going to share techniques that will help you overcome that issue. Setting up your camera, you will need an app that allows you to have manual controls of everything on your camera. The first thing is to lock in the ISO at 50, this is a very native ISO for the iPhone and will give you a grain-free image.

You have to set your frame rate at 24 frames a second. Most of us grown up watching movies in the movie theatres and what that taught your brain is that 24 frames a second look cinematic and now that so many people are familiar with these cinematic frame rates, the shutter speeds are where most people get it all wrong in my standpoint and here is why. Shooting at the proper shutter speed is a very crucial thing you need to get right in the beginning if you want to achieve cinematic looking footage. To find the appropriate shutter speed is very easy all you have to do is take whatever your frame rate is 24 and then multiply it by 2, you just double it. If you skip the step and shoot at whatever shutter speed your phone wants, your footage will not have the right motion blur to look cinematic, and it will end up

Looking way too crisp and that is not cinematic. If those settings are plugged into your phone, chances are your image will be too bright and that is where I use the polar Pro Variable ND filter system for my iPhone to bring it down. All you need to is clip it into your phone and then turn the filter until your image is properly exposed. It's very handy, and most importantly use incredible glass so that they don't compromise your image and as soon as you find the proper explode just click record.

The second tip is to learn how to move your iPhone in a way that replicates old cinema cameras and since iPhone is lightweight, it is very easy for you to move around and capture everything compared to the old big movies camera that is very heavy. To give your phone more stability and to capture your cinematic camera moves, you can use something like the polar pro hand grip. If you are not familiar with some of the traditional cinematic film moves, you can watch some videos online and learn some skills and practice along with it.

The final thing is in any film making process is to give your footage a cinematic color grid. With your iPhone, you can do the same. All you have to do is check whatever manual camera app you are using to see if they have a flat picture profile and by using a flat profile you can get more dynamic range in editing and also preserve more of the color and details that were originally there in your footage. You can now edit your iPhone footage in whatever desktop app you use to color your regular camera footage, or you can use Apple's already pre-made filters and then adjust the exposure, the contrast and the warmth, you will be surprise the quality of footage you can capture with your phone just by throwing an ND filter on it and using the proper settings. Follow these tips, and you are sure of filming a good quality cinematic video with your iPhone.

CHAPTER TWELVE

Night Mode

When using the camera app on the iPhone 11 pro max, the new Night Mode function will be automatically activated when the indoor or outdoor scene is dark enough to ensure brightness; this leads to natural colors and low noise. In short, new iPhone users should see an immediate improvement when shooting in low-light environments without having to adjust exposure settings.

If "Night mode" is suggested but not activated, the "Night mode" button appears at the top of the viewfinder and looks like a crescent moon. If you thought the scene would benefit from "Night

Mode," press the button - it turns yellow, and the number of seconds to exposure appears. If the lux level is below 10, the night mode is automatically activated.

When night mode is activated, the slider is displayed below the viewfinder, which you can leave at the time of the proposed exposure or manually select it. "Night Mode" automatically simulates long exposure for 1, 2, or 3 seconds. However, you can set this for up to 10 seconds, depending on the intensity of the ambient light.

When you are ready to shoot, click the shutter-release button, and hold the phone as far as possible because the camera simulates long exposure, and when you are done, you should get a picture that makes the camera look like it will look in the dark.

If you do not want to turn on night mode when shooting in extremely low-light environments, you can turn it off if you click on the yellow "Night

Mode" button when it appears at the top of the viewfinder.

Night Mode Comparison Between iPhone 11 Pro Max and iPhone XS Max

The new night mode of the iPhone 2019 and its ability to dim are what distinguishes the iPhone XS Max and the 11 Pro Max.

iPhone 11 Pro Max's night-time learning mode takes machine learning and multiple shots, even when you are close to black while preserving the color and feeling the night-time image.

The night mode is radically different from the best low light shots of the iPhone XSMax and allows iPhone users to take shots that could not be played on the iPhone XS Max.

Exposure to Night mode ranges from 1 second to 10 seconds, depending on the ambient lighting conditions, how long you store your iPhone, and much more, and this feature takes multiple collage shots to create a single image, so you need to make sure whether you have a fixed iPhone or stand.

These shots are not great for carrying objects like pets or children, and night-time photos are not always as bright when they are close to black, but they can take stunning looks.

As for the front camera, it has also been improved. It has a 12-megapixel lens (over 7 megapixels), and Apple uses the next generation of Smart HDR (also available for the rear camera), so the "beauty filter" that people hated on the iPhone XS Max, does not work. However, in good lighting, there is no difference between the snapshots on the front of the iPhone XS Max and the 11 Pro Max.

The front camera supports 4K speed at 60 fps and slow video at 120 fps at 1080p, allowing slow self-portraits, also known as "Slo-Fies." Another significant change to the front camera is the ability to take a larger image so you can zoom in or out as you like, perfect for group portraits.

Photographing Artifact

The Apple iPhone 11 Pro Max camera handles display subjects well, which is why the device scored high in the iPhone category. When viewing full-size images, the ringtone is visible along high contrast edges but does not usually cause massive distortions. The test found a few spots on some sample images, but the iPhone was generally in the pipeline.

While the iPhone lets you take great photos at the touch of a screen, there are several accessories available that enhance the shooting experience.

Photography Equipment

As you take photography more seriously on your iPhone, you might want to add some of these tools to your collection. It should be noted that one can very easily get trapped in the world of "gadgets" for iPhone photography.

Having one or all of these accessories will not instantly make you a photographer. Some items will give you more flexibility in creativity, while others offer a higher level of comfort.

1. Tripod

A tripod is an essential accessory you can have as a photographer - mobile or otherwise. A tripod is necessary for large exhibitions and self-portrait, but with so many options, how do you choose the best tripod for the iPhone? If you want to keep the "mobile" ideal of mobile photography, consider smaller and lighter versions that you can easily pack in your bag and carry with you.

2. Release the shutter

While you can certainly use an iPhone camera self-timer to give yourself time to self-portrait or minimize camera shake during high exposures, and even more effective method involves remote shutter release.

With the screen release remotely, you have even more control over the shutter reception because the timer settings do not limit you. You can take pictures when you're ready.

The most effortless remote shutter release came with your iPhone! So the EarPods that come with all new iPhone models include a built-in volume control button for your iPhone (especially for music playback).

However, as many camera applications allow the use of iPhone volume keys to control shutter release, this implies, you can use the volume controls with the same keys.

Plug EarPods into your iPhone before setting up a download (using a tripod), then press the "+" volume key to launch the shutter release.

Although using EarPods volume control is efficient and inexpensive, there is a significant disadvantage that EarPods templates that come with your iPhone are pretty fast, so you need to be close enough to your iPhone for this task.

In other words, this technique can be better suited for high exposure when you can stand next to your iPhone but want to minimize camera shake.

3. External battery/charger

If you usually have a full bag/backpack with a full gearbox, it would also be wise to carry a charger with a plug if you are in a cafeteria or other place where you have access to AC power.

However, assuming that you do not always have easy access to AC power to recharge your iPhone, you might also want to consider AC power that you can carry with you at any time for on-the-go charging.

Fortunately, as with tripods, there are many options available depending on your needs and budget. The simpler and cheaper external batteries will only charge your iPhone 1-2 times (if necessary) before it needs to be recharged.

But they are small enough to fit in your pocket, which makes them so easy to carry. The larger ones are still quite large, but you may want to keep them in your backpack or another bag as they will be a little too large to carry in your pocket.

Larger batteries/chargers can charge your iPhone up to 6 times before an external battery is charged; this can be exaggerated for most photo tours, but it can be a great advantage if you are going camping or otherwise will not have easy access to an AC charger for a few days.

4. Exterior lenses

A paramount way to bridge the gap between mobile and DSLR photography is to use one or more of the many spectacular lenses available.

One of the most popular options is Olloclip lenses. They are compact, easy to install and, deliver exceptional results.

If you want to improve your optics game, you might want to consider the option of premium lenses, such as moment lenses.

Additional options are available for extra lenses. As with every purchase of equipment, read as many reviews as possible before investing in other lenses to make sure you are satisfied with the purchase.

Finding a way to try different types of lenses with your friends is an even better way to buy educated shopping.

5. External light source

In low light conditions, the built-in iPhone flash can tweak. Most of us, however, experience their limitations - usually hard light, lack of energy regulation, etc.

An external light source usually provides better light quality, but also offers more flexibility to enhance your iPhone photo.

Although almost any light source can be used to illuminate the image, purchasing a dedicated light source specifically designed for photography will provide you with a more reliable and higher quality light source.

The advantages of a portable light source are generally:

❖ Adjusting the angle of the light source

• Adjustable power levels for better control of the light intensity

1. More even light distribution

❖ All these benefits will eventually make your photos more creative.

6. Mobile wireless disks

If you plan on taking lots of images in a short period, you may want to invest in an external storage device. Usually, these are flash drives (i.e., Still Parts) where you can upload your photos to free up memory on your iPhone.

It is easy to upload your photos to cloud storage as iCloud Photos, Dropbox, or Google Drive.

However, you must connect to a high-speed Wi-Fi connection or a large data plan from your mobile service provider. To backup your photos on the go quickly, the best option is an external storage device.

There are so many great options for these tools that freeing up available space would only take another link.

Keep in mind that wireless storage units are usually the most expensive of all the extras discussed in this article.

If you do not take hundreds of photos a day or plan an extended vacation where you cannot easily back up your photos, the wireless storage device may overload during regular use. Yet it is good to recognize them as an opportunity you may ever need.

7. Camera bag

Finally, you need something to bring this device, right? This decision does not have to be complicated because everyone does not have the right choice.

Many mobile photographers (including myself) pack their equipment into an existing backpack and don't think twice about it; it's a great place to start if you are packing a long day of photography for lunch, a rain poncho, or other items.

So take a DSLR camera or other camera to make it easier for your mobile camera to be in a camera bag with another device.

Instead, you may want to travel as lightly as possible with smaller items such as external batteries, other lenses, etc.

After all, it depends on your needs and goals. When taking pictures, try different bags (if you already have them) to see what works best.

Photograph Assistant App

When it comes to smartphone cameras, the iPhone 11 Pro has one of the best cameras on the market. It's so good that in recent years, some films made exclusively on the iPhone have become a headline. If you are among the people who no longer own a camera because the iPhone photos have turned out to be so great, you'll enjoy this list, as most users find that the iPhone camera is excellent, but not you have full control over the photos you take. And if you're a passionate photographer who owns a real camera, you will surely agree that you can't always bring them with you and sometimes have to make a smartphone. Whether you're an amateur or an experienced photographer, try these five best iPhone camera apps to optimize your photos instantly.

HALIDE

If you're an aspiring photographer, Halide may look a little confusing or fall out of your league; this gives you full control over the photos you take. If you have photographic knowledge and experience, you will be amazed because it allows you to make perfect pictures with your exact parameters - you can control everything from shutter speed to ISO. You can also view detailed information about how the camera handles data and settings.

OBSCURA 2

Obscura 2 is a simple and intuitive camera app for iPhone that allows you to take beautiful photos. This application will enable you to control multiple camera parameters with simple dials on the screen. There are also 19 unique filters that you can apply to your photos to give them a perfect look.

VSCO

VSCO is undoubtedly one of the best known and most popular camera applications. Millions of photos are taken and edited when published on Instagram every day. Usually, this app is only used to edit pictures taken with the standard iPhone camera app. With VSCO, however, you have far better control over your photos than with native camera apps. It is, therefore, worth trying. The free version of the app has some parameters that you can edit. However, Pro gives you complete control over your photos, and the fact that you can edit pictures without leaving the app is a huge bonus.

ProCamera

iPhone If you use your iPhone for frequent video recording, check out ProCamera. When it comes to photography, it has almost the same functionality as the app above, but with video, it's a whole different level. You can control the frame rate, resolution, HDR, stabilization, and more to create perfect videos.

CAMERA + 2

Camera + 2 is an ideal app for inexperienced photographers who want to learn and improve. This app is very similar to the native iPhone camera application but has a few additional buttons that you can use to improve the look of your photos without feeling overwhelmed by the multitude of buttons and parameters.

CHAPTER THIRTEEN

How iPhone 11 Pro Max New Technology Would Improve Quality of Photos and Videos Taken

The iPhone 11 Pro series is Apple's first smartphone equipped with a triple rear camera and at least a polarizer.

The triple camera series debuted on Huawei's P20 Pro smartphone last year and was quickly adopted by competing manufacturers.

The iPhone 11 Pro features a wide-angle camera as you would in previous models, but comes with the integrity of telephoto lenses with 2X optical zoom and ultra-wide image capture capability that captures multiple images.

Together these three cameras can create amazing portraits by photographing and mapping different depths to create a natural bokeh.

The amount of background blur and changing of the portrait lighting when the photo button is pressed using redesigned images on iOS 13, can be adjusted, so you can tweak any image and see the results in real-time.

LOOKING OUTSIDE

When using a telephoto lens with a dual camera and a wide-angle camera, the top and bottom of the camera become transparent; this allows users to see what is out of the frame by letting them know what they are missing and what is going to go into the frame.

SHOW IN DARK

The night mode works by taking a series of photos in different exposures and their approximation to create a bright and natural picture even in low light.

Night mode is automatically enabled and helps photographers capture more details without the need for a flash.

Small slow motion options

All four iPhone Pro cameras, including the front camera, can record video at 4K to 60 fps with extended dynamic range. Also, the front camera can take up to 120 frames per second for slower motion.

The iPhone 11 Pro, of course, has much more than its new luxury cameras. While the iPhone 11's basic phone is very similar to its previous predecessors, the Pro boasts significantly higher specifications to help the photos and videos you look even better.

The 5.8-inch OLED display has a massive 2 million: 1 contrast ratio (compared to 1,400: 1 in the base model) that turns black pixels into darker, deeper blacks.

Apple's TrueDepth display also adapts to ambient light to provide more natural colors by changing the white balance on display, which also reduces the visual effect when looking at blue lighting.

The software optimizations and the diverse editing features that Apple has included only improve the quality of photography.

The iPhone 11 Pro series is the first Apple smartphone to feature a rear triple-camera array.

The iPhone 11 Pro series features a regular wide-angle camera like you would have found on previous models, but the telephoto camera complements it with 2x optical zoom, and an ultra-wide that captures more in the frame.

SEE IN THE DARK

Night mode works when you take a series of images at various exposures and stitching them to create clear and natural images, even in dim light.

Night mode is turned on automatically and helps photographers capture more detail without the need to use a harsh flash.

SMOOTH SLOW MOTION SELFIES

All four of the iPhone's Pro cameras can shoot video in 4K up to 60fps with extended dynamic range; additionally, the front camera can also shoot up to 120 fps for smoother slow-motion performance.

Apple has branded these slow-motion selfie videos "Slo-Fies," although popular opinion sees this feature as a bit of fun rather than for any "Pro" use.

There is more to the iPhone 11 Pro than its fancy new cameras. While the entry-level iPhone 11 is mostly similar to its recent predecessors, the Pro model boasts significantly higher specs that help the photos and videos you take a look great on it.

The diagonal OLED 5.8-inch display has a massive 2,000,000:1 contrast ratio (compared to 1,400:1 on the base model) that turns off black pixels for more in-depth, darker blacks.

Apple's TrueDepth display also adjusts to ambient light to render more natural colors when you change the white balance of the display, which can reduce eyestrain when you stare at blue lighting.

The software optimization and versatile editing feature Apple has included on top of them only boost the argument.

Camera Hard Power

A range of ultra-wide-screen and telephoto angle cameras give you the chance to capture photos with 0.5x, 1x, and 2x optical zoom, also with 10x digital zoom.

In general, this is a massive improvement over previous iPhone cameras and better than the cheaper iPhone 11. With Apple's new Night Mode, it can keep up with the best competitors in shallow light conditions, while using iOS 13.2 deep fusion technology is closer than ever to the sharpness of a single-lens reflex camera with a large lens.

After Apple has been competing for the highly competitive camera for some time, Apple has been at the forefront of the iPhone 11 Pro series.

How to Take Better Pictures in Low Light

Although iPhones have always had a high-quality camera, low performance in low-light environments has been unpleasant for a long time.

When using night mode straight ahead, some professional advice can help you capture more exciting shots with the beautiful night sky.

Before continuing, it is vital to highlight the basic things about this automatic setting.

When the iPhone detects a dark environment, Night mode automatically appears in the Camera app. A crescent icon appears at the top left of the screen to confirm that it is available for use. When it is active, the on-screen timer (next to the Night mode icon) automatically starts counting down the exposure.

It uses a new sensor, machine learning algorithms, and the Neural Engine A13 processor to capture clear images at night.

1. Make sure your iPhone stays stable

First, make sure you keep iPhone as stable as possible when taking night shots on the iPhone 11 series. Do you wonder why you need to do this? Many things are happening behind the scene before and after taking a photo.

When night mode is activated, iPhone cameras first analyze the amount of light available. After quickly analyzing the existing light, they select the desired number of shots to take the picture.

After the initial operation, the cameras take a series of images at different exposures for a specified period. Smartphone not only allows you to highlight all relevant aspects but also catch the best parts.

Finally, the dominant chip analyzes all captured images and aligns them perfectly by eliminating blurry photos. Finally, all the images seamlessly combine. As a result, a brighter image appears.

While all these things happen in the background, you should keep the iPhone stable; to make things a little easier, optical image stabilization plays a vital role in reducing vibration.

Ask how long do you need to hold a smartphone? It only depends on the surrounding environment. Shooting may take up to 5 seconds or may take a few seconds. You can watch the timer that appears next to the Night Mode icon to see how long you need to leave your device unchanged.

2. Manually control night mode

Manually control the night mode effect on iPhone 11 Pro Max If you want to try night shots or get better images, you can control the night mode effect manually. Although the default is 5s, the temporary connection can be up to 30 seconds long.

To adjust the exposure, move the slider (above the shutter button) left / right. When shooting, the slider temporarily fully counts down to the end of the exposure to keep you in the loop.

3. Better Pictures

The darker the surroundings, the longer it will take to take pictures. Although it may sound a bit unpleasant, especially when you want your footage to appear quickly.

Setting a more extended time in the dark can help you take better pictures with many details of the night sky; this is usually not possible with shorter exposure. If your device's camera takes longer to take pictures, you don't have to worry about the delay. Instead, look at the opportunity for better images.

4. Use wide-angle to shoot

With the iPhone 11 series, you can use night mode for both telephoto and wide-angle cameras because they support optical image stabilization.

Note that it does not work with the ultra-wide-angle camera as it does not offer OIS support.

Night mode works effectively with the telephoto lens, but the wide-angle lens is used optimally. So if you want to take a better picture, make sure you use the wide-angle camera as it is a better lens.

5. Use a tripod

As already mentioned, a series of photographs are taken in night mode. And the technology used behind the scenes is very similar to the long exposure. So you can apply the night exposure's long exposure technique fully to get better results.

Although the device uses OIS (Optical Image Stabilization) and software to reduce blur, it sometimes does not deliver the desired result. To take better pictures, use a tripod. It can play an essential role in removing the blur, allowing the device to make more impressive images.

It may sound a little bad for head-rush, but you get much better pictures of the night sky. In short, to take a lovely photo of the night sky, a tripod is a better choice.

6. Make sure the items are stable

From experience, I can say that night mode works much better when the subjects are stable; this is because the device has to take multiple photos and put them all together. The less movement, the better your images.

So don't be surprised if your smartphone doesn't take a better picture of your active pet or running child. But if they can remain stable for some time, you can make cute night portraits of pets and people.

7. Night mode may not work correctly with every shot

Note that night mode may not work correctly for each photo. Sometimes you see colors that are too dramatic to accept. At other times, the high contrast may seem a bit strange. Not to mention that it sometimes looks covered in exaggerated shadows.

When it comes to photography, a few professional tips can make a big difference if implemented correctly. So be sure to try them if you want to take perfect selfies or attractive photos.

Using the HDR Features

HDR (High Dynamic Range) camera helps you take great photos in high contrast situations. The iPhone quickly captures several images at different exposures and combines them to give your photos more light and shade.

The iPhone uses HDR (rear and front camera) when it is most effective by default. For best results, keep your iPhone stable and avoid moving objects.

- Turn off HDR automatically

4. The iPhone automatically uses HDR when it is most effective by default. To manually manage HDR, follow these steps:

- Go to Settings> Camera, turn off Smart HDR. Then, on the camera screen, touch HDR to turn it on or off.

1. To enable HDR from the camera screen, touch HDR, and then on.

CHAPTER FOUTREEN

Photography Tips

Tip 1. Take Slofie Video (Slo-Fie)

How to shoot Slofie on iPhone 11 Pro Max and take slow-motion selfies on the newly acquired iPhone 11 series. When moving Slo-Fies, first turn on the selfie mode with a regular camera, then switch to slow motion.

Tip 2. Update your photos

You can reshape pictures captured on your iPhone to fit objects into a random frame. To do this, go to Settings - Camera - to switch to "Photo / Video Captured Frame." You can now take photos with a TV lens or a conventional wide-angle lens. When you edit and crop an image, you will find that the image is slightly more full than the picture taken.

Tip 3. Take ultra-wide-angle images

Click the "0.5" mark above to take extra-wide shots.

Tip 4. Get wide selfies

Initially, you can shoot an only advanced selfie, but with the iPhone 11 series, you can extend the frame to take more photos in each selfie. Just click the extension arrow above to add more to your selfie.

Tip 5. Capture fast-moving videos

Quick-Take is the first new feature in the iPhone 11 series, and you can shoot swift videos without having to switch to photo mode. Just lock the shutter and swipe right to shoot the video.

Tip 6. Furry portrait

Now you can also shoot portraits of furry friends. Your portrait is no longer limited to catching people.

Tip 7. Click on the other tools below

To use these tools, you can switch from the lock or directly to the arrow at the top screen.

Tip 8. Photo filter

With some exquisite camera filters, you can take great pictures on Instagram. Just click the arrow at the top of the camera screen, then click on the primary color icon to the right.

Tip 9. Expand the portrait

Take a full portrait on your device. Just click the 1x icon to the left of the frame, and your frame will be more comprehensive.

Tip 10. Switch to the telephoto lens

Switch to ultra-wide-angle, wide-angle, and aperture lenses on the iPhone 11 Pro Max using a radial-scale wheel. Now, if you shoot ultra-wide and ultra-wide-angle images, you should also try large teletype lenses. As well as extra-wide images, you also have access to a "2x" telephoto lens above the shutter.

Tip 11. Change the aspect ratio

You can also adjust the aspect ratio if you access the camera tools by clicking the arrow at the top of the screen. And pressing the 4:3 ratio, this will open up the possible aspect ratios for you to choose.

Tip # 12. Low light shooting at night

Night mode is a deliberate feature of the camera, and it has finally appeared in the iPhone 11 series.

Tip # 13. Expand Panorama

If your photos can be full, why can't panoramas be full? Just click on the button above "1x".

Tip # 14. Don't forget to blow it up

Last but not least, "continuous shooting," you can take burst photos by merely locking the shutter. You need to press the shutter button and the left button to get a continuous picture, and you should hold this position until you get the required number of photos.

Ultra-Wide-Angle Tips

1. Open the camera app as usual, either directly from the program itself or the lock screen

1. Touch the button near the shutter button "1x" or "0.5" to change to an ultra-wide-angle lens

5. Insert your picture and take a picture, usually by clicking the button

- Ultra-wide photos are stored in Photos and all other photos taken on the iPhone.

1. You can also choose between 1x and 0.5x camera variations, press the "1" or "0.5" button, and then use the focus to manually adjust the focal length anywhere between the two lenses, such as "0.75" or "0.6".

1. If you are already familiar with using the 2x optical zoom for iPhone Plus and iPhone Pro, you should be familiar with using ultra-wide-angle camera lenses, since this process is

mainly focused on selecting the focal length.

1. With iPhone 11 Pro Max, you can switch between 0.5x, 1x, and 2x.

- Ultra-Widescreen Camera Whether iPhone is available in any orientation, vertical or horizontal, you can also use the iPhone with ultra-wide-angle lens video.

1. The result of ultra-wide-angle camera photography is, as expected, much more comprehensive than a conventional iPhone lens with ordinary camera photographs.

- Ultra-wide viewing angles make things smaller but include more room for photos; this allows greater efficiency than zooming.

Smart HDR Tips

The iPhone HDR works best when a photo is taken with the phone in a three-way mode; this means you can't take HDR photos without a tripod. However, if you are not using a tripod, a firm hand in HDR shooting is essential; this is because HDR does not capture movement well. Because iPhone's HDR combines three different shots into one, excessive movement can cause many photos to look incorrect. For the same reason, shooting moving objects does not work. You can experiment with HDR and get weird shots in double exposure, but for HDR, the movement is at the expense of the shot.

HDR is best used in high contrast scenes. Here are some examples of HDR usage:

1. Landscapes: HDR can capture the light of the sky and the darkness of the earth in one

shot, which does not cause very dark or excessive sky.

1. Objects directly in sunlight: The sunlight shades and creates a wide range of contrast in the photo. Using HDR adds balance to all elements, light, and shade.

4. Backstage scenes: The same principle above applies to the opposite situation. If you have a bright scene in the background, HDR shines in the foreground, externally and without washing.

Deep Fusion

Apple's Deep Fusion camera technology has been described as "computing crazy science" in the iPhone 11 assembly.

Deep Fusion is a sophisticated image processing system that uses the A13 Nerve Motor to capture images with significantly better texture, detail, and reduced noise in low light conditions. It has no user-centric signal that Deep Fusion is used because it is automatic and invisible.

This feature will not be used when using an extremely wide lens, the "Out of Frame" mode, or when shooting a series.

Before you press the shutter button, it takes nine shots that have already taken four small shots, for seconds. When you press the shutter button, you get a long exposure, and then within a second, the Neural Engine analyzes a fused combination of long and short frames. To choose the best of them, select all pixels and pixels per pixel and spend 24 million pixels on optimizing detail and low noise; this is the first time a neural processor is over-responsible for creating an output image. It's computational photography of mad science. "

To use the Deep Fusion camera mode:

- Make sure you have updated iPhone 11 Pro Max to iOS 13.2

1. Then go to Settings and then Camera

1. Now make sure that the download mode outside the download mode is off.

❖ Make sure you use a wide-angle or telephoto lens

❖ Deep Fusion now works behind the scenes when shooting

Long Exposure

Long exposure is a technology that is usually only available on DSLRs and expensive high tech cameras. Many travel enthusiasts view Instagram, posting their beautiful photo for the long haul.

Running a long exposure on the iPhone.

Step 1. Launch the Camera application.

You can open the iPhone's camera from the lock screen (Swipe left), the camera icon on the screen, and use the 3D Touch quick-action options (You can touch the app icon room).

Step 2. Now turn on the On Photos Live settings (tap the three concentric circles at the top of the screen to enable the Live Photos feature). If you have already activated, then it looks yellow instead of white.

Enable Live Photos and click on the shutter to make Live Photos on iPhone iOS 11

Step 3. Now set the focus of your camera lens to capture background animations and release the shutter button.

Note: The best result suggestion - you need to use a tripod or place your phone in the usual place where you are not shaking your iPhone. The rebound ratio to speak of will not give you a good exposure result.

Night Mode Tips

When you open the Camera app on your iPhone in a dimly lit room, you'll automatically see the selected night mode button. Hold your hand as far as possible, and touch the shutter button to capture the image. Depending on how dark it is, it will take a few seconds for the process to complete, so keep stretching.

5. Open the Camera app.

- Prepare the composition for the photo you want to take.

Touch the Shutter button.

1. Keep your hand firm when taking the photo. You will see a timer that knows how long and how long you are.

1. Touch the thumbnail of the photo in the lower-left corner to see how it looks.

2. Open the camera, touch the shutter, tap on the thumbnail

1. When you press the capture button in Night mode, a slider timer will appear to display the number of seconds it will take to capture the image. The timer will count as long as the camera is fixed. If you stumble too much, the camera will alert you and remind you to keep it.

How to Manually Change the Night Effect Level:

5. Open the Camera app.

1. Prepare the composition for the photo you want to take.

5. Touch the Night mode button when it appears.

4. Slide the timer switch to the right or left to choose between activating Night mode, keeping it at the default time, or maximum time (often 9 or 10 seconds).

1. Open the camera, press Night mode, scroll

➢ Touch the capture button to capture your image. Hold your hand until the timer counts.

➢ Touch the thumbnail of the photo in the lower-left corner to see what it was.

➢ If you drag the slider to the maximum exposure time but have your iPhone in your hand, you can't get a perfect shot. Remember that this Night mode uses an open shutter to capture more brightness, which means that every movement is also recorded. If there is too much movement from your unstable hand, there will be nothing strong enough to connect the camera.

How to disable Night mode:

Night mode automatically switches to low light areas. It's like you have auto-flash turned on. The iPhone 11 or iPhone 11 Pro will determine whether night mode should be enabled and how long each exposure should be. But if you don't want to use Night mode, you can turn it off.

➤ Open the Camera app.

• Touch the night mode icon in the upper left corner next to the flash icon. The icon will turn gray when you wish, then take your picture.

Picture Editing Tips

After taking a picture, open it in Photos and touch Edit. You can then adjust the size, angle, lighting, add filters, etc. to the photo. Choose an adjustment, such as Brightness or Saturation, and swipe to change the intensity, if you are not satisfied with your new changes, click Cancel to revert to the original format.

Panorama Mode

- Launch the Camera application on your iPhone.

- Swipe left twice to change the mode to Pano.

- If necessary, press the arrow buttons to change the capture direction.

- Launch the camera, swipe left twice, or press Pano

- Press the shutter button to start taking a panoramic photo.

- Rotate or move your iPhone or iPad to capture as much of your surroundings as possible. Try to align the tip of the arrow with the yellow guide. If you move too fast or too slow, the app will also give you feedback.

- To end the panorama, press the shutter button.

Grid

The 'grid' helps you get a straight shot when you accurately adjust the perspective of your alignment. To access the grid:

• Go to settings

• Camera

• Turn on the grid

Tips:

1) Double-check the edges of the image to ascertain it is parallel to the grid lines so that the image can be shot directly.

2) Check the left and right lines at the same time to make sure the screen is not tilted.

3) Place your shot at the juncture of the gridline to get a full photograph.

Monochrome Light Mode

The new Monochrome Light Mode is an extra high-brightness feature in iOS 13 that fills the blurred section with pure white, for a completely white background image. Not only is the image cleaner, but it also has a high-level feel for studio shooting.

Tips:

1) Turn on high-light monochrome mode when shooting, instead of setting after shooting.

2) Slightly move or expect a perfect monochrome image of the theme and background.

3) The theme and background colors may not be particularly close. There is a specific contrast to get the perfect picture.

Dynamic Photos

Focus on shooting, take dynamic photos.

Tips:

1) Shoot at night.

2) Turn off the night scene mode.

3) Press the trigger as you move with the moving object.

4) Choose a scene with a lot of backlights to make the effect more natural.

CHAPTER FIFTEEN

Photography Similarities Between iPhone 11 Pro Max to iPhone XS Max

From a pure hardware point of view, all the cameras on the iPhone 11 Pro Max are better than the cameras on the iPhone XS Max. The primary wide-angle camera has a larger sensor that allows more light, the telephoto lens now has a larger aperture of f / 2.0, and there is a camera with a very wide-angle (f / 2.4) that was not there before.

However, in practice, there is not much difference between wide-angle comparisons of camera shots taken with iPhone 11 Pro Max and iPhone XS Max in the right lighting conditions.

iPhone 11 Pro Max is, in some cases, clearer with more vibrant colors, but there are times when certain areas of the image stand out more than the iPhone XS Max. Image quality may change between the two phones later this year when Deep Fusion, the new iPhone 11 feature, appears.

Machine learning is used by Deep Fusion to process images per pixel, improving noise, texture, and detail.

For portrait mode, edge detection in iPhone 11 Pro Max is similar to edge detection in iPhone XS

Max; with this, you will see much difference in well-lit shots in a good light.

However, there are new features in portrait mode that are worth highlighting. Now you can take wide-angle portrait shots with a 1x lens next to the telephoto lens, so you can get more shots if you like. The telephoto lens itself has been improved, so shooting in low light will turn out better.

The iPhone 11 Pro Max features an ultra-wide-angle camera that is brand new and lets you shoot more full shots than is possible with the iPhone XS Max. In comparison, the ultra-wide-angle camera offers a focal length of 13 mm, while the wide-angle camera is 26 mm, and the telephoto lens is 52 mm.

The new focal length, which is about 13mm, makes a world different from landscape and architecture photos and can be used creatively to take close-up pictures with unique perspectives. An ultra-wide-angle lens is an excellent addition to a smartphone and can be more useful than even a telephoto lens.

The ultra-wide-angle lens has an f / 2.4 aperture and no optical image stabilization like other lenses on the iPhone 11 Pro Max, so it doesn't work as well in low light, and the images are not as sharp but perfect in the right light as well abroad.

All three cameras are available for video recording and recording, and you can change them at will with the new camera switch.

With wide-angle lenses, the real difference between the iPhone 11 Pro Max and the XS Max is the new night mode and low light mode of the iPhone 2019.

The iPhone 11 Pro Max uses a camera and multi-shot learning to create useful photos even when close to black while retaining the color and feel of night photography.

Night Vision is dramatically different from the low-light highlights of the iPhone XS Max and allows iPhone users to take photos that won't fall into the iPhone XS Max.

Nighttime reports range from 1 second to 10 seconds depending on ambient lighting conditions, how long you still hold your iPhone, and more, and this feature uses multiple combined shots to create a single image, keep it iPhone fixed or use a tripod.

As for the front camera, it has also been improved. There's a 12-megapixel (up to 7-megapixel) lens, and Apple uses the next-generation Smart HDR (also available for the rear camera), so a filter that the iPhone didn't like for the iPhone XS Max. But with good lighting, there is no tone difference between the facade of the iPhone 11 Pro Max and the XS Max.

The forward-facing camera supports 4K at 60 frames per second and slows 120fps video to 1080p, allowing for slow-motion selfies, called "Slo-Fies." The other significant change to the front camera is the wider shooting option so you can zoom in or out, which is ideal for selfies groups.

Camera Commonality of iPhone 11 / 11 Pro and 11 Pro Max

Night mode

Night mode, as a new feature, allows the iPhone 11 to automatically capture light, even in low light, to capture bright, beautiful photos. Put, this is possible due to the high performance of the "A13" processor in the iPhone 11 series.

To take beautiful photos in dark places, you must keep the shutter open to capture more light than usual. However, if the times are long, the images will be very blurry.

In the iPhone 11 series, many photos are downloaded automatically and instantly, and the pictures don't blur, the result is a bright, unmatched photo.

Night mode is the first attempt in iPhone history. The iPhone camera had a poor impression of recording at night, but this time it also seemed to raise the issue of "Android machine performance exceeding."

Advanced portrait mode

Portrait mode is a shooting mode that makes the subject stand out with instability in the background.

The iPhone 7 Plus has improved this feature but has evolved further into the iPhone 11 series.

The significant change is that you can now take black photos with a pure white background. No matter where you shoot, the background will be described, which will give you a studio look.

By changing the light intensity applied to the subject, you can create the shade you want. Plus, you can easily capture beautiful photos because the shooting mode is custom made for the subject.

New generation intelligent HDR

Smart HDR is a feature that haply combines the right parts of photos with different exposures in one picture.

In short, it is a feature that combines many photos with different brightness to create a beautiful picture. Function similar to the night mode described above.

The iPhone 11 comes with enhanced next-generation "smart HDR" that allows for more accurate image processing. Adjust the boundary between subject and background and pixel-by-pixel noise.

With this feature, you will not be afraid of overexposure or under-execution. It's a feature that makes you want to shoot in different situations and try out the iPhone 11 camera.

TrueDepth camera capable of capturing 4K video

The TrueDepth camera reads facial movements using the camera, such as Face ID and Animoji.

With the iPhone 11 Series TrueDepth camera, the camera's display area is expanded. A great photo without a sticker will make the picture more fun.

Also, this time, you can shoot a slow-motion selfie called "slow-motion. Only using slow graphics will make you feel that your standard of living has increased by one step.

Also, HD has the highest picture quality, but the iPhone 11 series can shoot 4K video!

Not only has the image quality been improved, but editing, zooming, and cropping can also be done.

Videos are straightforward to use, such as filming videos on YouTube and creating a welcome video clip.

Triple camera performance

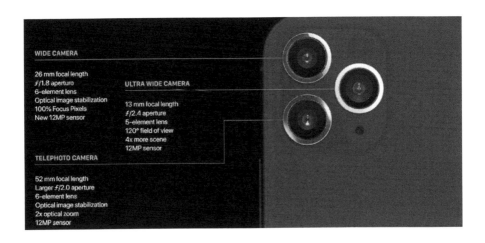

The main difference between a dual camera and a triple camera is the presence or absence of a telephoto lens. The iPhone 11 and iPhone 11 Pro / 11 Pro Max consist of the following lenses.

Wide-angle lens

Ultra-wide-angle lens

Telephoto lens

The performance of wide-angle and ultra-wide-angle lenses is typical in all three models, so the difference is the presence or absence of a telephoto lens. The telephoto lens of the iPhone 11 Pro / 11 Pro Max tool lets you narrow down the target area.

Usually, the larger you zoom in, the lower the image quality, but don't worry about the iPhone 11's telephoto lens. Since it's a zoom lens only, the image quality remains the same even when you zoom in.

With the addition of a telephoto lens, it can now be used instead of a camera lens or a reflective lens.

Optical image stabilization and dual optical image stabilization

There are differences in the level of camera shake correction.

The iPhone 11 has optical image stabilization, while the iPhone 11 Pro / 11 Pro Max has dual optical image stabilization. Dual optical image stabilization is a feature that is only installed to the max, such as the iPhone X and iPhone XS / XS Max.

Since both lenses have image stabilization, they are challenging to see, and you can take beautiful photos. The size of image stabilization varies, but if you don't want to get rid of it, you can have a triple camera.

Can the iPhone 11 Pro Max Replace SLR Cameras?

The iPhone camera has a reputation for being as good as an SLR camera. The triple camera on the iPhone 11 Pro Max is phenomenal.

Camera performance

The "F" value, which indicates the number that light can record, can be set from 1.8 to 2.4, and you can adjust the brightness and the degree of blur.

Also, the smaller the numbers, the brighter and dimmer they are, so you can shoot like a professional photographer.

Price

If you try to buy a reflective lens with the same level as the iPhone 11 series, the cost will be $ 1700 for the lens itself and $2500-3500 combined with the central unit.

As the cheapest iPhone 11 64GB can be purchased for $850 (excluding tax), this is an astounding cost saving. Even the iPhone 11 Pro 64GB with a telephoto lens costs $1200, so it's cheaper to replace the lens.

Convenience

Because SLR cameras change lenses depending on the shooting scene, you must purchase at least two or more lenses.

But with the iPhone 11 Pro Max, you don't have to change lenses. Wide-angle and telephoto lenses are reflected in real-time.

Also, this automatically reflects the optimum distance from the subject, so that even amateurs can easily capture professional-quality photos.

Weight

Single-lens ignition cameras, together with the body and lenses, weigh at least 600g-1000g.

The iPhone 11/11 Pro / 11 Pro Max weighs less than half, making it easier for women to hold. You can take photos anytime, anywhere, without worrying about "the camera is heavy, and you leave it at home in the end."

With all these features, it's no exaggeration to call the iPhone 11 Pro Max a camera, not a smartphone.

Strengths and Weaknesses of iPhone 11 Pro Max

Strength Points

- Triple camera with three powerful cameras for sharp picture and video with super-telephoto angle and telephoto zoom

- Night camera mode, which captures bright images even in complete darkness

- New 12 MP Selfie Camera for Holiday Selfie and Enhanced Video Features

- Photo features that use artificial intelligence to improve shots and improve the post-processing

- Powerful A13 processor, which doesn't even require video editing and still image editing problem

- Many productive features for the iPhone

- ❖ Fast charging function with matching charging accessories

- ❖ High compatibility with third parties and their extensive accessories

Weak points

- ❖ The price, which can be more than 1000 dollars for many models

- ❖ iPhone design is a little old

Travel Photography with iPhone 11 Pro Max

It is becoming increasingly clear that smartphones are in no way inferior to classic digital cameras. In some cases, where comparative photos were taken, smartphone recording was found to be superior to an SLR or mirror camera in terms of professional photography criteria such as exposure, color authenticity and depth of field.

If you're taking a photo of your album at home as a vacationer or traveler, today's smartphone from big, established manufacturers is enough. Especially with sharp pictures of the iPhone 11 Pro Max, there is almost no need to pack an extra digital camera.

Travel photography with the iPhone 11 Pro Max is so advanced that, at least in theory, you can always take great smartphone photos on your vacation; this is still a bit unusual for many users, as they have been using a reflective lens camera or mirrorless system for high-quality photos for decades and cellphone photos are more inferior. These hours are definitely above the new generations of smartphones.

If smartphone photo opportunities continue to improve so fast, conventional digital cameras must quickly become a specialized product.

Combined with a stabilization smartphone, the iPhone 11 Pro not only produces crisp video - but it also shakes it.

High-quality travel equipment is a must, especially for all people who are active tourists and travelers. These include numerous leisure devices such as high-quality headphones, aerial photography and professional video recorders, tablets such as the iPad Pro, smart camera, smartphone (stabilizer) such as DJI Osmo Mobile 3 (test) and of course a smartphone such as iPhone 11 Pro Max, which combines many features and can be used on-site mainly to provide travel information and navigation to a vacation spot.

CHAPTER SIXTEEN

How to Activate the Photo Feature

By default, the feature is enabled for video only (more precisely: for fast video capture). You can set them for photos as follows:

- ❖ Open the settings and click "Camera."

- ❖ There are three paths under the "Composition" category.

- ❖ Enable Photo Out of Frame.

2. If you then take photos, there is more information about the image, for example, when you straighten or cut portions of a pattern in the picture.

Note: Even if the function is enabled, it still depends on external factors, regardless of whether the function is used during recording. If this worked, you could recognize it in the gallery by an icon that appears in the upper right corner of the corresponding photo. It has the shape of a square with an asterisk. To view the additional area, open the image in the photo app, and select "Edit." If you now press the crop tool symbol, you will see the full size.

How to Capture Square Photos

If you want to see the entire photo without having to click and open it, the square box will help you capture the right perspective without having to take and shoot later.

When you first launch the application, you see an arrow at the top of the screen instead of other controls. Click this arrow, and you will see the options appear above the download button.

From these options, look for an option that says 4: 3. If the option has been changed before, it may have another value, such as 1: 1 or 16: 9.

This option will be expanded to give you all the different proportions you can use to take photos. Press 1: 1 to select the square format.

You will see that the viewfinder will fit in a square format. You can now take photos with this 1: 1 ratio.

In this format, you can switch between two or three lenses on the iPhone 11. The camera lens selection is not relevant to any particular aspect ratio.

Photo Advantages and Disadvantages

MERITS

4. Rich in detail in most test conditions

5. Direct exposure and wide dynamic range in most cases

- Fast, precise and repeatable autofocus

4. Vivid and pleasant colors

1. Super wide-angle lens with great detail and dynamic range and control of the right color aberrations

1. Zoom performance at near and medium intervals is sufficient

DEMERITS

- Significant noise in all lighting conditions

- There is noise on the telephoto position

- Effects of calling on external images

- Flash photos have no details

- The intense yellow color is cast in low light

- The pictures on the screen are not in detail and seems to be noised.

Video Advantages and Disadvantages

MERITS

- Wide dynamic range

- Fine exterior and interior details and well-regulated noise

- Bright and pleasant colors

- Effective against vibration

DEMERITS

- Jitter effect while recording while walking

- The internal white balance is unstable

- Autofocus shows clear traces during viewing

- Alias artifacts can sometimes occur

CHAPTER SEVENTEEN

SIRI

Siri is a programmed voice that helps you perform a particular task just by asking it to; it is like a robot you can talk to and command. When you speak to Siri, it is a quick way to get things done; report on the weather, you can tell Siri to translate a phrase, find a location, set a timer, and more. The more you use Siri, the better it becomes familiar with your needs.

However, to use Siri, the iPhone must be connected to the internet, which may incur charges from your cellular provider.

Siri is set up when setting up your iPhone for the first time, but if somehow you did not set it up, you can still do so, launch the Settings app, tap Siri &

SEARCH, then press the side button for Siri, or turn on Listen for "Hey Siri."

You can summon Siri with your voice; say "Hey Siri," then ask Siri a question or to do the task for you. E.g., you can say, "Hey Siri, set the alarm for 8 pm." To ask Siri another question or to perform another task for you, tap the colored circle.

You can prevent the iPhone from responding to Siri, place the iPhone face down, or go to settings and turn off Listen for "Hey Siri."

If you cannot speak to Siri, you can type to Siri. To do so, follow the steps below;

2. Launch the Settings app, then tap ACCESSIBILITY, select SIRI then turn on to SIRI.
3. You can request by summoning Siri, then use the keyboard and text field to ask Siri any question or to accomplish a task for you.

Find Out More about Siri

There are other amazing things Siri can do, use Siri on iPhone 11 Pro-Max to get information and perform tasks.

Here are some things SIRI can do;

- ***Find answers to your questions:*** You can find information on the web, get sports scores, get arithmetic calculations, and many more on SIRI.
- For example, you can say, Hey Siri; I want to know what causes the rainbow, Hey Siri, can I see the derivative of the cosine x.
- ***Perform tasks with apps on iPhone:*** You can use Siri to control apps with the help of your voice; for example, you can say, "Hey Siri, set up a meeting with Michele at 4 pm". When the onscreen response includes

buttons or controls, you can tap them to perform further tasks.

- **Translate languages:** You ask Siri what languages it can translate; it would give you a list.
- **Play a Radio station:** Say something like, "Hey Siri, tune in to WAZOBIA 95.1."

Letting Siri Know More About You

When you let Siri know more about yourself, including things like your home and work address, relationship, and more, you can get personalized service. You can say something like "Send a message to my wife" and "FaceTime Dad."

Tell Siri who you are, to do so, open the contacts app, and fill out your contact information, launch the settings, tap SIRI and SEARCH, select my information, then tap your name.

You can teach Siri how to pronounce your name, say something like, "Hey Siri, learn to pronounce my name," you can as well tell Siri about your relationship, you could say something like; "Hey Siri, Diana Lindsay is my wife" or "hey Siri, Henry Cavil is my uncle."

Know More about Siri Suggestion

Siri can make suggestions on what you might what to do next, such as; confirm an appointment, send emails, and how to use your apps.

As Siri learns your routines, you may get suggestions for just what you need, at that particular period, for example, maybe you usually order pizza on Fridays, Siri might suggest you order it near that time. If you get a call from a private number, Siri might detect who is calling; although it is based on numbers saved in your emails.

Siri can help you select names of movies, locations and everything viewed recently on your iPhone; you can tell a friend that you are almost at a place, Siri will give you the estimated time of getting there.

Siri also introduces the website and information into the search field as you type. Since Siri knows the topics that interest you most, this is suggested in the news.

To deactivate Siri's suggestions, start the Settings app, tap on SIRI & SEARCH and disable the following list.

- Search suggestions
- Looking for suggestions
- Lock screen suggestions

For a specific app, tap the app, and then see suggestions for Siri.

Use the Siri Function in Your Car

With Carplay or Siri Eyes, you can focus on the road by making calls, playing music, sending text messages, getting directions, and other iPhone features with Siri.

Carplay is only available in selected vehicles. It does the tasks you want to do on your iPhone while driving, and you can view them on your built-in screen. Carplay uses Siri, so you can ask Siri what you want.

With SIRI EYES FREE, which is available in selected cars, you can use your voice to control features of your iPhone without looking or touching the phone.

To connect iPhone to your car, make sure the Bluetooth is on, to summon Siri, press and hold the command button on your steering wheel till a voice sounds, then say your request.

CHAPTER EIGHTEEN

Family Sharing and How to Set It Up

Family sharing is an exclusive feature in the iPhone used in connecting families together, with family sharing, up to six members of a family can share iTunes Store, App Store, and Apple Books purchase; an Apple Music family membership; an Apple new+ subscription; an Apple arcade subscription; Apple TV channels subscription and many more.

To be able to use family sharing, one adult or eldest (known as the organizer) of the family member chooses features for the family to share and invites up to five members to participate.

When family members join, family sharing will be set up on their devices automatically.

Family sharing will require the organizer to sign in with his Apple ID, to confirm the Apple ID you used for the iTunes store and the rest.

To set up family sharing, follow the simple steps below;

2. Launch your settings >[your name] then select SETUP FAMILY SHARING
3. Select the features you want to share, here are some below;

- iCloud storage
- Apple TV+
- Screen Time
- TV channels
- Location Sharing
- Purchase Sharing

- Apple News
- Apple Arcade
- Apple Music

4. Follow the on-screen instructions to sign up.

To accept an invitation from another family or wants you to become a member of the family sharing, Tap accepts in the Invitation.

You can leave family sharing at will, but only the organizer can stop the family sharing, to leave family sharing, follow the steps below;

2. Launch settings App> [your name] Family sharing > [your name]
3. Choose leave family
4. If you are the organizer, tap stop Family sharing.
5.

Sharing Purchases with Family Members

If your household members share the iTunes Store, the App Store, and the Apple Bookstore, they are all centered on Apple's ID culture. Once the item is sold, it will add to the company's history and distribute sales throughout the family.

To access items purchased from the iTunes Store, open the iTunes Store, secure it, and then select Purchase. Select a family member, in the list, select the purchased image and click the download tab.

To access sales from Apple Books, open Apple Applications, print your profile picture at the far right, select a family member, and then select a section. Click on any book or purchase, and then click the menu next to the purchased book for download.

Ask To Buy Feature

If your family sharing group shares purchases, you can, being the organizer, require that young family members request approval for purchases or free downloads.

Follow the steps listed here to do this;

2. Launch your Settings app>[your name], select Family sharing
3. Tap the name of the person who needs a request for approval, then activates ask to buy.

Hiding Purchases

As the organizer, you can as well hide your purchases on the iTunes Store, App Store, and Apple book store.

To activate hide purchases, do the following;

2. Launch your Settings app>[your name] > Family sharing
3. Select purchase sharing, then deactivate 'share my purchases.'

Find a Missing Device

A family member can help locate another family member missing device if he does this before it got lost:

- Turn on Location Services: open the Settings app, tap Privacy, then turn on location services
- Turn on Find my iPhone: open settings app, tap 'find my,' select find my iPhone, then turn on 'Find my iPhone,' enable offline finding and send the last location.

- Share your location with family members: launch settings, open family sharing, select location sharing, and then turn on share my location.

Now if you did the above before the iPhone got lost, perform the below to locate where it is;

1. Launch Find My on your iPhone
2. Sign in with your Apple ID.
3. In the list of devices, select the one you want to find.

Your device will be on top of the list while your family member's own will be below yours. The selected device appears on a map so you can see where it is.

CHAPTER NINETEEN

How to Connect Bluetooth Devices

Bluetooth devices can be connected to iPhone 11 pro-max; many Bluetooth gadgets can be connected to the iPhone; some are; headphones, speakers, car kits, AirPods, and more.

You can turn on your Bluetooth by launching the Settings app and tapping on BLUETOOTH, then tap the switch to activate.

To quickly disconnect Bluetooth from devices without deactivating it, open the control center, and tap the Bluetooth icon.

Before you can fully connect a device to your phone using Bluetooth, you will have to pair, to pair a Bluetooth device, follow these procedures below;

2. Put the device in discovery mode by following the instruction that comes with the device.
3. Open settings app on your iPhone 11 pro-max, tap Bluetooth.
4. Tap the device in the Bluetooth device list to pair and connect.

IPhone should be within 33 feet (10 meters) of the Bluetooth device.

You can also un-pair a device, to do this, follow the procedure below;

2. Launch the Settings app, then tap the Bluetooth.

3. 2. Tap the circle icon next to the device, then tap FORGET THIS DEVICE

Make sure Bluetooth is on while un-pairing devices.

Use the Earpod

Apple earpods features Microphone, volume button, and center button, the center button is used for phone calls, audio and video playback and Siri, even on a lock screen.

Here are some things you can control with your apple ears:

- Pausing a song or video: Tap the center button to pause a song or video, or tap again to resume playback.

- Jump to the next song: Double-click the middle button quickly.

- To return to the previous track: Quickly click the middle button three times (this only works for audio playback.

- Answer an incoming call: Click the middle button

- End current conversation: Click the middle button

- To reject an incoming call: Click and hold the middle button until two low tones confirm that you refused the call.

- Siri: Click and hold the middle button until you hear a beep that alerts you.

See image below

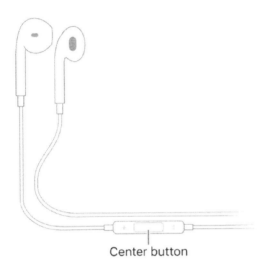

Center button

How to Use Universal Clipboard

Copy and cut content (either a block of text or an image) and paste it somewhere else or on another iPhone, iPad, or a mac; for the universal clipboard to work while pasting on other devices, you must be signed in with the same Apple ID on all the devices. You must be connected to WIFI, be within Bluetooth range, Bluetooth must be turned on handoff must be enabled. The copied content should be inserted within a short period. To copy, cut and paste content, do the following;

- Copy: pinch and close with three fingers
- Cut: pinch and close with three fingers two times
- Paste: pinch and open with three fingers

However, you can also tap and hold a selection, then Tap, CUT, COPY, PASTE.

How to Use iPhone 11 Pro Max as WIFI Hotspot

iPhone can be used as a Wi-Fi hotspot for any other device, to provide internet access to them, use instant hotspot with other devices, you must be signed in with the unchanged Apple ID across all the other devices. To make your iPhone instant hotspot available to others, follow the procedure below;

1. Launch the Settings app; tap WIFI on your other iPhone or iPad.
2. You will see your iPhone network, choose your iPhone network.

When your devices are signed in with one Apple ID, the password would not be required, but when you are connecting the iPhone hotspot to other devices that are not apple-related, a password will be needed to access the iPhone internet connection.

If you do not use the hot spot, your device will disable to save battery life.

If you are not making use of the hotspot, your device will disconnect to save battery life.

Connecting iPhone 11 Pro Max with Your PC Using USB Cable

Connecting your iPhone with PC, you will need a USB cable, once iPhone is connected to PC, you can use it to do any of the following;

- Transfer files
- Sync content
- Charge the iPhone
- Share the iPhone internet, and many more.

When you want to connect your iPhone with a PC, make sure you have one of the following;

- Mac with a USB port and OS X 10.9
- PC with s USB port and windows seven.

If you have any of the lists above, depending on the type of computer you are connecting to, then you can connect iPhone to your computer using the included USB-C to lightning cable. If the iPhone does not connect to your computer, do one of the following;

- If your computer has a USB-C port, use a USB-C to lightning cable or USB-C to USB adapter to connect.
- If your computer has a USB port, use a lightning USB cable.

See image below:

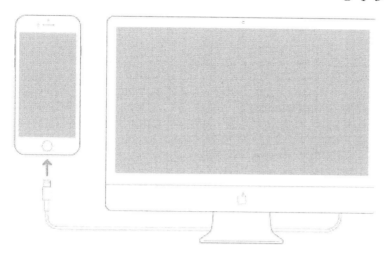

How to Sync Your Device with PC

You can make use of your iPhone to sync the listed items with your pc; Albums, songs, podcasts, movies, TV shows, audiobooks, books, photos, videos, contacts, and calendars.

Sync lets you update these things between your computer and iPhone.

(Note: If you used iCloud or other services, such as Apple Music, sync options for your computer are not available.)

Follow the process below to sync your iPhone to your Windows computer;

1. Connect your iPhone and your computer with the USB-C lightning cord

2. Find iTunes on your computer by clicking the iPhone button in the upper left corner of the iTunes window

3. Select the sidebar type of content you want to sync (movies, books, and more)

4. Select synchronization to enable synchronization for this type of object.

5. Repeat steps 3 and 4 for each type of content you want

6. Add on your iPhone, then press apply.

By default, your Windows computer syncs with iPhone when you connect it.

How to Transfer Files from Your iPhone To PC

You can transfer files to your computer from your iPhone when you connect them using the USB-C lightning cable, to transfer files with your windows PC, follow the procedures below;

2. Connect iPhone to your PC using the USB-C lightning cable.

3. Locate iTunes on your Windows PC, click the iPhone button near the iTunes window.

4. Click file sharing, then select an app in the list, then do one of the following;

- *Transfer a file from your iPhone to your computer:* choose the file you want to transfer in the list on the right corner, click "save to" decide where you want to save the file, then click "Save to"

- *Transfer a file from your computer to your iPhone:* click add, choose the file you want to transfer, then select "Add."

You can delete a file from your iPhone through your PC by pressing the delete button, then confirm by clicking delete.

Files transfers show immediately, to see the list of items sent to your iPhone, visit the on my iPhone found in the Files app on iPhone.

CHAPTER TWENTY

Three Ways to Configure a New iPhone 11 Pro Max

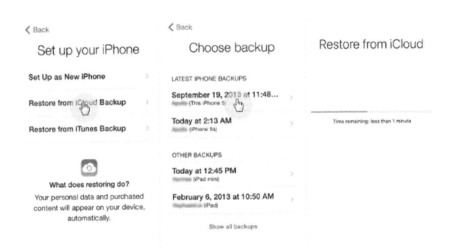

You can configure a new iPhone in one of three ways, start, restore from another iPhone or import content from a non-Apple phone. Here's what each of these options means in more detail.

- Define it as now - it means everything starts - every parameter - from scratch; this is for people who have never used a smartphone or online service before, or want their iPhone to feel genuinely new.

- Restore from a previous backup of your iPhone, iPad, or iPod touch - you can do this online with iCloud or via USB using iTunes; this is for people who have a previous iOS device and switch to a new one who wants everything on their old device not to be affected by the new device.

- Import from BlackBerry, Windows Phone, or Android - Apple has an app on Google Play that supports Android, but online services allow you to move large amounts of data from any old device; this is particular to people switching to an iPhone or iPad from another mobile platform.

Conventional Steps to Set Up iPhone 11 Pro Max

- Tap the image to configure and start with your finger across the screen.

- Select your language.

- Select your country or region.

- Select a Wi-Fi network. If you are not within the range of a Wi-Fi network, you can add it later. Instead, select Mobile.

Right now, you can choose to use automatic configuration to configure a new iPhone with the same code and password settings as another iPhone. If you decide to install the latest iPhone manually, follow these steps.

- Click Continue Reading after reading Apple's data and privacy.

- Touch Skip Location. If you do not want to enable services at this time, select Skip services, you can manually enable certain location services, such as Maps.

Configure Face ID

- Launch the settings from the home screen.

- Tap Face ID and Password.

- Enter your password.

- When you open it, click on ID and password

- Click "Set Face ID" (or "Set a different look" if you have set a Face ID).

- Click Go.

- Move your head slowly for the first scan.

- Create an access code. You can create a standard 6-digit passcode or create a 4-digit passcode or a custom passcode by clicking Access Code Options.

- A question would be asked to know if you want to restore as a new iPhone, set backup, or move data from Android.

How to Set up iPhone 11 Pro Max When Restoring a Backup

If you do not want to start using a brand new device, you will want to port data from your old iPhone to a new one or transfer data from your old Android device to your new iPhone. Here's how.

Restoring a backup from iTunes or iCloud

It is time to decide how you want to port data from the old iPhone (if you are starting from scratch, find out how to set the iPhone as new). When you restore apps and data from another iPhone, you have two options; iTunes or iCloud.

The one you choose depends on you backing up your old iPhone to iCloud or connect it to your computer and back up using iTunes.

The key is to make sure that your old iPhone is backed up first.

After backing up the old iPhone, choose whether to restore your new iPhone from iCloud or iTunes.

Steps to Set up Your iPhone 11 Pro Max from Scratch

If it is your first iPhone and you do not want to move your Android data anymore, or you are your tenth iPhone and want to start over, you can set your iPhone as new.

- Tap 'Set as a new iPhone.'

- Enter your Apple ID and password. If you don't, you can create a new one. Click Do You Have an Apple ID? And follow the instructions.

- Read and accept the Apple Terms of Service.

- Click Accept again to confirm.

- Configure Apple Pay.

- Choose iCloud Key.

- Set up Siri and "Hey, Siri."

- Click Send Diagnostic Information to Apple when applications are crashing, or other problems have to occur, or click Do Not Send if you do not want to submit.

- Turn on the Zoom view for a more accessible view.

- Tap to get started.

How to Set Up the Apple TV App

Using the Apple TV app, you can watch Apple TV+ other originals as well as your favorite TV shows, series, movies, sports, and even live news. You can subscribe to any Apple TV channels such as HBO and ShowTime, watch titles from streaming services and cable providers; you can also purchase movies or rent TV shows.

You can subscribe to Apple TV+ (**NB:** This is not available in all countries) and watch apple originals without ads.

To subscribe to Apple TV+, do the following;

- Launch the Apple TV app
- Select watch Now, scroll down to Apple TV+ row then do one of the following;
- Get 1 Year Free Apple TV + Subscription: Choose NEW 1 Year Free (Available for Apple ID Authorization)
- Start a 7-day free trial: Select APPLE TV + Free (Available for Apple ID Authorization) Apple TV + offers a free trial per subscriber or family.
- Start a monthly subscription: Tap to subscribe.

1. You should review your signature information and then confirm with Face ID, Touch ID, or Apple ID.

The Apple TV app may be associated with the utility. For the first time from a supported app, tap Connect to the Apple TV app to find out. One amazing thing you can do with the Apple TV app is to add your cable or satellite service to your Apple TV app. Single sign-on provides immediate access to all supported video apps in your subscription package.

To add your cable or satellite service to the Apple TV app, follow these steps below;

1. Launch the Settings app and tap on TV PROVIDER

2. Select your TV provider, then login with your provider details.

However, if your TV provider is not listed, sign in directly from the app you want to use.

How to Set Up Cellular Service

The cellular connection only works with a SIM from a carrier; you will have to reach out to your carrier to set up a cellular plan.

How to insert and install the SIM as been taking care of, in previous chapters, so we will talk about how to manage your cellular plans in this segment

When setting up your iPhone, you can select how the iPhone will use any other line if you need to change the settings later, do the following listed;

1. Launch your Settings app, and tap CELLULAR then do the following.
- Select your cellular data, then select a standard line. Enable the Allow cellular data switching for iPhone option to use all lines that depend on coverage and availability.

(NB: additional costs may be charged if the data is roaming and you are outside the area covered by the railway network)

Tap the default audio line, then select a line.
When you make calls from another device, e.g., from your Mac, to your iPhone with dual SIM, the call is made using the voice line.
Instant Hotspot and Personal Hotspot use the selected line for cellular data.

Connecting To the Internet

There are only two significant ways of connecting your device to the internet that is, connecting via a cellular network or connecting through an available WIFI connection.

To connect iPhone to a WIFI network, follow these simple steps below;

1. Launch the Settings app
2. Scroll to WIFI, then turn on WIFI
3. TAP one of the following
- *A network:* Enter the password, if required
- *Others:* This allows you to join a hidden network, in which you would need to provide the network's name, security type, and password.

If the WIFI icon appears at the top of your screen, the iPhone is connected to a WIFI network.

To connect to your cellular network, please follow the simple steps below;

Usually, your iPhone automatically connects to your carrier's cellular data network if a WIFI network is not available. If the iPhone does not connect, check the following:

1. Verify that your SIM is activated and unlocked
2. Go to settings and TAP cellular
3. Verify that cellular Data is turned on

Learn Some Basic Gestures

You can control your iPhone and its apps using simple basic gestures; in this segment, we will be looking at some basic gestures such as; Tap, touch, and hold, swipe, scroll, and zoom.

❖ **TAP:** Touch any finger lightly on the screen

❖ TOUCH AND HOLD: Touch and hold an article in the app or control center to view content and take quick action. On the home screen, touch and press each application icon to open a short menu.

❖ SWIPE: Quickly move your finger to the screen

❖ ZOOM: Swipe your finger on the screen, spread it to zoom, close it to zoom. You can also duplicate an image or website twice to zoom and flow twice to zoom. When you're on Maps, double-tap, and move, then drag it to zoom, or count to zoom out.

❖ SCROLL: Move your finger to the screen without lifting, touch the screen again to scroll.

Wake and Unlock

The iPhone automatically closes the screen when it's not working, saves you time, and sleeps when you're not using it. You can quickly get up and open your iPhone if you want to use it again.

To get up and open your iPhone, do one of the following;

❖ Press the Home button to wake up your iPhone 11 pro-max

❖ Use the Face ID feature to wake up your iPhone 11 Pro-Max, just by looking at it; you wipe it from the bottom of the screen

❖ Click the Home button and enter your passcode if needed.

How to Restore Your Device to Factory Setting

To restore the iPhone's factory settings, you can use a Windows PC to clear all iPhone data and settings and install the latest version of iOS.

If you restore the iPhone's default settings, all data and settings will be erased, but before you remove the iPhone, it is recommended that you back up important files and data, so when the iPhone is removed, you can restore the files as shown in the last segment.

Follow these steps to restore your iPhone with Windows PC;

1. Connect the iPhone to your computer with a Lightning USB-C cable
2. In the iTunes application on your PC, click the iPhone button near the top window
3. Click summary

4. Click restore iPhone.

5. Follow the on-screen instructions

Warranty

iPhone 11 Pro-Max carries a two-year warranty, which is the same as the iPhone XS; it offers 2-year protection, including accidental damage.

CONCLUSION

This user guide is a complete handbook for users who just got the iPhone 11 pro-max. However, it can also help beginners who have not used any iPhone series before. iPhone 11 pro max is a durable and sturdy phone; you are sure getting a great battery life, swift and efficient display. You would have a superb user experience while taking advantage of its unique shooting performance, which is one of the most desirable thanks to the primary camera; the bottom line is that iPhone 11 pro max is worth it because 'its got the right amount of everything.''

ABOUT THE AUTHOR

Pablo Mendoza is a geek and very passionate about photography and technology, a fan of Apple and all its devices. He loves to travel and reach every corner with the camera ready to capture the moment.

Printed in Great Britain
by Amazon

43900808R00167